Christmas Time

Douglas B. Whitley, Jr.

Copyright © 2012 Douglas B. Whitley Jr.

All rights reserved.

ISBN: 1490581561
ISBN-13: 9781490581569

DEDICATION

To my friend, Dr. Billy where the Christmas stories started.

CONTENTS

	Acknowledgments	i
1	Christmas Knight	1
2	Cowboy Christmas	Pg. 15
3	Doc Taylor	Pg. 47
4	Christmas Light	Pg. 59
5	Outback Christmas	Pg. 95
6	Christmas 1944	Pg. 123

ACKNOWLEDGMENTS

Thank you, my beloved for keeping the Spirit of Christmas all the year.

1 CHRISTMAS KNIGHT

The castle stood tall and strong against the bleak December skies like an island in a sea of snow. The banners fluttered gently from the keep stirred by the seaward breeze. It was snowing. Great heavy flakes floated softly from the sky and settled on the castle, the sea and the lone rider who sat easily astride his mighty charger just beyond the castle moat.

The great black stallion shifted, shook his head and blew silver ghosts from his nostrils. Andrew patted his neck and quieted him with easy words: words that belied Andrew's thoughts. There were tears coursing silently down Andrew's cheeks. Giles had been his knight. Was his knight, for he was gone now: his body lying in state in the silent chapel where Andrew had spent his lonely vigil. Andrew had been his squire. His thoughts flashed again to the ambush. The horse pranced sensing his anger. The Normans, the hated conquerors. Three of them had attacked Giles and Andrew in the wood. They had thought the fight was three against one until Andrew's strength and skill had shown him he was a swordsman with which to be reckoned.

He had dispatched his opponent and turned to see Giles fell another when he felt Giles go down. They had been back to back in the snow of the deep woods fighting for their lives. Giles slowly sank to the ground, his blood staining the snow crimson.

Then Andrew heard the raucous laughter of the third Norman. The Knight's face burned with hatred, his eyes bright with blood lust.

"I'll save you for another outing, young Saxon, though you will provide no more entertainment than your valiant knight awash in his own blood. Beware my blade should our paths cross again young whelp."

And he was gone. His laughter rang through the woods with the retreating hoof beats of his horse. "Take me home, Drew, home to Father, home to Iana, home to die." Giles had whispered. "No! No, you'll be all right. Be quiet now," Andrew spoke softly, but in his heart he knew Giles would not live. The damage was too great. Lovingly he eased Giles upon his horse holding him as they rode together, Giles blood leaving a dripping trail as the horse walked the trail of trodden snow. Slowly they made their way back home. There Giles died in Iana's arms with words of Andrew's bravery upon his lips and so Andrew had been knighted. Iana presented him with Giles' spurs and armor, tears flowing down her face falling on her swollen belly. She was great with child. "That it were not so. I would give up spurs and shield for Giles' return."

His voice broke the silence of the winter's eve. He nudged his horse forward and crossed the moat into the castle yard. A groom took his stallion and Andrew made his way into the great hall, his fur cape brushing the flagstones beneath his boots. There it stood, tall, beautiful, proud, a great fir tree in the center of the hall. It was Christmas.

The thought broke like a shattered vase inside him. He and Giles had fetched the tree, laughing and joking, throwing snow, not as knight and squire, but as brother and brother, for so they were.

Now his brother was gone, gone from a wife he loved, a child who would grow tall without him. The three of them had mourned. "Take comfort, my son, Giles is with our Lord Christ now. He is safe and without pain. Take comfort, daughter from the God of all comfort. We do not sorrow as those that have no hope." All these thoughts rushed at him as he stood beside the tree holding back the tears.

The druid's tree, or so the tales went, but his father had said they would keep Christmas in the old ways. The tree will remind us of the cross, his father had said, and so it was. The Christmas celebration was only days away. Midwinter's eve had passed. Christmas. Christmas with its Yule log and holly, with stews and puddings, capon and partridge, boar and venison. Tables magnificent with candies and sweetmeats. All in the evening after a day of hunting.

With presents to remember the wise men's gifts although Father said the wise men weren't there the day of the Child Christ's birth. Then there would be hunting after an early fast breaking with the mid-day meal in the woods beside a great fire. There was hunting with hawks, deer drives. Each man waiting for the magnificent hart to crash through the bracken. Finally there was the boar hunt with spears. Each hunter on foot. It was only this last year that Andrew had gotten his first boar and Giles had born him home triumphantly on his shoulders. How they had laughed. Now it would be no more. Giles' life had been taken, stolen. The greatest gift of all had been snatched from him by the enemy for sport, for the pleasure of killing. Christmas would never be the same.

The nights were long and the days passed slowly as the celebration grew nearer. His father, Cedric, Sir Cedric, a knight and chieftain in his own right had gathered his retainers and friends for the occasion. Most had come for the funeral and stayed to comfort the family. Time hung on Andrew like a leaden weight.

Finally Christmas day came. Many had sought to dissuade Cedric from the hunt, but the good old man would not deprive his guests from their sport for his grief. Life must go on he had said and so the festivities began.

Sir Cedric prayed as they sat in their saddles. "Lord, honor this, our celebration of the day of Your birth, Your incarnation.

May our hearts be pure and our lives clean for Thy sake. Comfort us in our grief and give us a forgiving spirit toward those who seek to persecute us. Let us remember on this day, of all days to have peace on earth and good will to all men. Amen". There were over a hundred there, landholders, ladies, friends of the family, cousins, aunts, uncles. Many from Andrew's past that in other years had shared many a jest. But not this year, his heart was not in it. Andrew kept to himself amidst all the laughter and stories of other years, other hunts. Iana stood by the gate as they rode out, her expectant belly obvious even under her fur cloak. She waved them off, but no smile broke her lips. Voices were quiet as they passed her, but then, the sport began. Andrew sat the mount and rode out with the others, but his spirit had affected his falcon and it would not fly. He was in no mood for this. It brought back too many memories. The laughter of others shattered against the grief in his heart. He gave his bird to a servant. "Yes, Sir Andrew," the man had replied.

Sir Andrew, the title burned like gall in his throat for what it meant. Andrew rode alone through the deep woods to grieve letting the horse pick his own way through the evergreens shrouded in snow. The saddle leather creaked and the harness metal jingled in the silence of the forest. Even the steps of the great stallion were muffled in the quiet snow. Only the breathing of the animal broke the stillness.

Too still, too quiet. There was someone near. He could no longer hear the noise and laughter of his father's guests. "Well, my little friend, you have come a long way in so short a time. Did you jump into the empty saddle of your dead knight?

How convenient for you. I have done you a great service." The blood drained from Andrew's face as he heard the mocking distain in the Norman voice. "I will kill you for what you have done" roared Andrew. "No, it is I who will do the killing, my little friend, but I want to know where to take your body. I am Donatien de Dupree, and you are, Sir Knight?" Sir Andrew of Hastings, second son to Sir Cedric, the chieftain here." "And where is the first son?" "You have murdered him" Andrew growled. "What a pity," sneered the Norman, "Sir Cedric will lose both his sons in so short a time. And Christmas too! Guard yourself as best you can young one." Andrew's sword sang as he drew it from its sheath. The two horsemen bore down on one another in a fury. They met as their great stallions crashed through the bracken and the clamor of their swords echoed through the silent forest.

Peal after peal like a great bell rang the meeting of their blades. On they fought in the clearing. Suddenly Donatien reached for Andrew's foot and flipped him from his saddle. Donatien slashed at Andrew's head. Andrew blocked the blow and with a mighty sweep of his sword wrenched Donatien from his horse.

On they fought, the ringing of steel on steel filling the air. Again and again the Norman swung his blade and each time Andrew blocked the killing blow. Suddenly Andrew parried the Norman's weapon, pivoted and caught him full in the side with the edge of his blade blood pouring from the wound. Donatien faltered, his eyes wide, and collapsed in the snow. Andrew stood on the Norman's sword arm raised his weapon for the killing stroke. He wanted to watch the light go out of the Norman's eyes. "Wait! Wait, my son, do not do this thing!" You have defeated him that is enough. Killing him will not bring back Giles. "An eye for an eye" is that not what the Latin scriptures say Father?

Vengeance is mine, I will repay" Andrew spat the words. "Vengeance is mine, I will repay, saith the Lord. It is not ours to claim, but His. If you kill this man, you are no better than he" spoke his father softly. Andrew gripped his sword tighter. He raised it high and plunged it into the ground at the fallen knight's side. He fell on his knees and began to weep, his rage turning to bitter tears. "What would you have me do, Father?" "See to his wounds. Forgive him and give him the gift of life. It is the greatest gift of all. It is what Jesus has given us. Forget it not, my son. Bind his wounds, bring him home. He shall be welcome. Andrew did as his father said, remembering as he bound the wounds his brother, Giles and the trail of blood that followed them.

"What do you, Saxon? Why do you not finish me? Do you seek to spare me to make sport of me with your dogs? Why do you not finish me as I would you were you lying here?" "My father does not wish for you to die. Not by my hand, not on this Holy day." A hardened smile curled about the pale lips of the Norman. "You wish to ransom me? My family will pay you well. Take care of me; my life is of great worth to you." Cedric knelt slowly by the wounded man. "Young knight, your ransom has already been paid. By one you do not yet know. We will take you to my hall where you may mend." Loss of blood closed Donatien's pale lips. He breathed one careful breath and lost consciousness. The hunting party made their way back to Cedric's long hall with Donatien's body pulled slowly on a make- shift bier. Andrew riding, leading Donatien's horse. The black gloom after the red rage of battle enveloped him like a mist. His anger slowly died to embers. Runners had gone ahead to alert the healers of their return. Iana was in the gateway barring the passage. "I forbid this murderer the house, Father. I will now allow Giles killer to enter here." In an instant she drew the jeweled dagger that had been Giles present to her a year ago. She raised it high above her hear. Donatien opened his eyes. He heard the voice. He saw the dagger begin its descent.

Even as Iana began to move pain shot through her. She dropped the knife and fell to her knees cradling her belly. The baby was coming.

Quickly Andrew picked her up and strode with her into the hall. Cedric motioned the bearers on their way. People were running here and there.

Iana's cries of childbirth were mixed with the screams of Guy's pain as the healers began to see to his wounds. The day passed. All thought of Christmas gone. The guests moved in and out of the great hall like sleepwalkers. They ate what was at the table. They gathered in small groups to speak in hushed whispers near the braziers. Women rushed to fetch water from the hearth. Toward evening the small defiant cry of a new born was heard in the hall and people began to smile again. Andrew had spent the day by Donatien's side. Held there by anger and doubt. Anger at the death of his brother; doubt that he could hold such hatred in his heart. As fatigue enveloped him he let go of his hatred and fell to his knees. "Abba Father, Holy and Glorious one, Creator of heaven and earth forgive me my hate. Forgive me my anger. Help me to love as You have love. Help me to forgive as You forgive. Help me, Father." Peace flooded his heart. He rose and knelt beside Donatien's bed. He took some water and sponged Donatien's forehead. He pressed a little to his parched lips. Tears slid down his face as he did so. Slowly Donatien's eyes opened. Confusion, awareness passed over him like a cloud. "Where am I? Why am I not dead? Why have you spared me?" "My father spared your life. You are here in our home. Your wounds have been tended.

You are forgiven." "Why? Donatien whispered. "It is our way" Andrew answered. "The Saxon way?" "No, it is the way of those who follow Christ, who seek to do His will. Forgive me my hatred, my anger." The Norman slowly shook his head, his eyes staring in disbelief. Sir Cedric came softly into the room. "How are you faring, young knight?" "He is recovering, Father," Andrew said. "We both are. The healers say that though the wound is deep it was caught in time. Not much blood lost. They think he will survive." "That is well then." Donatien struggled to speak. "You said my ransom had been paid. What did you mean?" "Do you have the Latin, young knight?" "Yes." "Then here is your ransom "[16]*sic enim dilexit Deus mundum ut Filium suum unigenitum daret ut omnis qui credit in eum non pereat sed habeat vitam aeternam"* In the French it is thus [16]*Car Dieu a tant aimé le monde qu'il a donné son Fils unique, afin que quiconque croit en lui ne périsse point, mais qu'il ait la vie éternelle.* In the English it is God loved the world He gave his only Son that whosoever believes on Him will not die, but have life eternal." Jesus the Messiah, the Christ paid your ransom." Then as if a curtain had been drawn or a veil lifted Donatien began to understand. "Forgive me, forgive me! He cried. "You are forgiven. Even as God the Father has forgiven us in the death of His Son, so you are forgiven for my Giles. Remain here until you are well enough to move.

Then we will see you to your home. If you wish to send a message, if you have wife or family we will send someone to let them know where you are and what has happened." Sir Cedric told him. "There is no one. I have some friends here and there, but no family in Britain. They are all in France and it has been long since we spoke though they would have paid a ransom to save their heir." "Then be our guest and heal."

Iana lay quietly with the baby in her arms. He was sleeping on her breast. There was a soft tap at the door and Sir Cedric entered. "How is it with you, daughter? And with my grandson? What will you call him?" "His name is Nevan." She whispered. "Sacred. That is a good name. He is sacred before the Lord. And you, my child? Is it well with you? Or will you nurse your child on the bitterness in your own breast? I saw your eyes as you were about to strike. Eyes filled with anger, hate." "That man killed my love, my only one. Am I supposed to act as if he did nothing? Am I supposed to welcome him into my home with open arms?" "Forgiveness is a hard thing for us and yet the Lord God Almighty abjures us to forgive. 'Forgive us our sins as we forgive those who have sinned against us.' I have lost a son, you a husband. I have wept with you. My heart also has been filled with anger as yours. There was a moment when I heard the story and saw the blood of my son that had I held a blade with that man before me I too would have done as you, but then I reflected on my own sin.

Those whose lives I have taken, in battle yes, in defense of home and hearth, yes, but still a life taken. Over that I cannot rejoice. And so my own heart forgave and so I too received His forgiveness. If you cannot forgive this man your heart will be filled with a bitterness that will poison you, your child, perhaps all of us. 'Let no root of bitterness grow in your heart and by it many will be defiled.' Think on this my child. You have my love and prayers. Rest now." Sir Cedric left as quietly as he had come. Anger and hate welled up in Iana's heart as well as hurt and sorrow. Her life and love had spilled out with Giles blood. A part of her had died with him.

Great heaving sobs began to wrack her body. The baby woke with hunger and began to nurse. In her mind she saw her bitterness flowing into his young life. Her heart broke with the thought of what he might become with such poison filling his soul and she too began to walk down the road to forgiveness of the one she sought to kill. The day passed and she began to grow restless. She dressed and wrapped up the sleeping Nevan and began to walk the great hall. She found herself at Donatien's room. She knocked and Andrew opened the door to her. His brow furrowed and he blocked the way. "All is well, Andrew. I have not come to kill him. Please, I must see him. "Andrew stepped back and bade her enter. Iana saw a man the age of her Giles, but one who even in his sleep had a hardness to his face that told his story.

Andrew stoked the brazier in the room and pulled up a the heavy oaken chair for Iana beside the bed. She sat and began to slowly rock with tiny Nevan in her arms softly crooning to him. They sat together for a time and then Donatien slowly began to stir. A wave of pain shot across his face. He gasped and then he woke with a start. Andrew pressed water to his lips then wine mixed with a little poppy. Soon the pain began to ease. "Have you come to kill me, Lady?" "No, I have come to ask for your forgiveness." "It is I who am in need of that. Hatred has ruled my heart for many a year and I have given it free rein. It was in hatred that I killed your good husband and sought to end the life of Andrew here. Such kindness as has been shown me I have never known. Such kindness I have never expected never deserved. I have thought long here in this bed of my life, my evil. Forgive me, Lady, if you can find such forgiveness in your heart from one who has wronged you so mightily." "You are forgiven, but I too must ask for your forgiveness. My heart was filled with anger and hatred as well. Forgive me, my lord." "How can I not when so much has been forgiven me?" "Then all is well, my lord." "My lady, what is your name? ""Iana," She smiled for the first time. It means God forgives." And with that smile Andrew knew he had gained back all the Christmases he had lost now and for the rest of his life. The bitterness would not poison them all.

It was healed as Guy was healing, as Iana was healing, as he was healing as well. It was a Christmas to remember with sorrow and with joy for each realized that Christmas was a time of peace and goodwill to all men who are at peace with God.

The End.

2 COWBOY CHRISTMAS

It was cold. Jesse was wrapped in everything he owned just to keep warm. He had old sacking on his feet and legs. He could just feel the reins through his sheepskin choppers and he must look pretty strange with a cut up old blanket wrapped around his head over his hat to keep his ears from freezing and his nose from falling off. His horse couldn't be much warmer knee deep in the wet snow; the tethered pack mule following resignedly behind. Cautious step by cautious step they made their way through the tree line hoping to find shelter. He knew there was a tie hack's shack somewhere nearby. Whether he could recognize it in the snow was something else. Jesse didn't want them to find his frozen body atop his frozen horse with a frozen mule when the tiehacks came to cut rail ties in the spring. He had been making the circuit on the holdings just checking on things for the railroad. They owned just about everything; the rails, the trees, the land, the lives. He saw some rabbit tracks in the snow ahead of him and began watching to see where they led. "Might still be around." He thought. "Couldn't be too old to still show in this snow. Yeah, there he was hiding in plain sight by staying still." "You just stay still a bit longer." Jesse thought to himself. He eased the colt out of its holster and slowly brought it to bear on the rabbit.

The blast roared and the red spattered the snow crimson. He rode up to the carcass and stepped off his mount. Hoping he wouldn't sink to his waist in the snow.

He grabbed the limp animal by the hind legs and threw it over the saddle horn. Getting back up on his horse was harder with his feet wrapped up, standing in the deep snow but he made it. He gave his mount a tap with his heels and they plunged forward slowly like wading through deep water. He saw the shack. Its angles at odds with the blanketing snow over the roundness of the boulders nearby. It wasn't much. Maybe eight feet by ten put together with logs chinked with mud, a level roof of small pines with some flat rocks to hold it all together. It would hold his heat and keep out the worst of the cold. The small overhang would have to be enough for his animals. He cleared some drifted snow enough for his horse and the mule to stand free. He threw down some fodder from the mule's back. He grabbed the lantern and some oil, lit it with a match so he could see. He eased open the rickety door hoping the leather hinges wouldn't come apart. "Well, it's dry," he said to himself. There was a platform built into the wall to keep a body off the ground and a hand sawn stump for a small table. It was better than sleeping out in the weather. He had enough provisions for a fortnight. He'd only been out a couple of days. There was a storm building. He might just sit it out here.

Not much between here and the ranch if he got caught out in the weather. It was almost Christmas. Not that it mattered much to him. No family. Rachel and Jacob were long gone: killed by some rebel deserters while he was away fighting the Yankees. That was the last year of the war, just before the surrender at Appomattox. He had been running ever since. Running is what brought him to Wyoming. It had taken him twenty-five years to get here. He was still running, but he was running out of places to go. It's hard to run when the thing you're running from is inside you. He skinned the rabbit, collected some squaw wood and built a fire. He watched the smoke roll softly through the hole in the corner of the roof. The heat felt good. He took a small sip from his canteen. He began to peel off the layers that had kept him warm. It needed to dry. He needed to eat and sleep. The cold stole the heart as well as the heat out of you. Jesse had felt it draining out of him all day along the trail. He had enough food to last, but tomorrow he might hunt. Just for something to do. He ate the rabbit, washing it down with more water. He finished unpacking the horses. Wiped them down with some of the sacking went back in, wrapped himself in his bed roll and slept.

He made coffee over the small fire and wrestled with buffalo jerky for breakfast not sure who would win.

The snow had continued to fall over night and it was even deeper than the day before when he went out of the shack to check on the animals. He had heard some elk bugling not too far away and he thought he might like to find them. He wrapped himself up against the cold, strapped the snowshoes to his feet and began to ease his way through the trees, looking, listening. Elk were one thing, wolves were another and he wanted to make sure he was the hunter, not the hunted. He knew there were grizzly bears here as well but they should all be safely asleep in their dens. As he moved and listened his mind returned to the past. It was always with him. The war, the death, the pain, the running.

Slowly he was working to get the wind in his face; he stalked through the trees searching for game. It was in the silence after moving from behind a tree to a boulder the size of a buffalo that he heard the snort of an elk. It carried far in the cold stillness of winter in Wyoming. He stopped and began to search for the animal. His gaze moved farther and farther away until he spotted the majestic beast in a small clearing two hundred yards ahead. He slowly brought his Winchester to bear and sighted down the iron sights of the long blue barrel. He took a deep breath, steadied himself against the rock, both eyes open. He slowly squeezed the trigger until the rifle leaped in his grasp as the bullet exploded from the barrel.

Christmas Time

The elk jumped with the sound, but even as he did the bullet caught him in the shoulder and passed through the heart. He was dead in an instant. Jesse levered the casing out of the rifle and picked up the warm brass putting it in his pocket. He shoed to the elk and began to dress it out. He took the hide, the antlers and as much meat as he could carry knowing the wolves, the coyotes, and the pine martins would have the rest. It was late afternoon with darkness falling fast that he made his way back to the shack by the trail he had marked along the way.

At the cabin he threw a rope over a tree branch, tied on the sack with the meat and raised it up out of grizzly reach hoping they were all safely hibernating for the winter far away from him. He cooked the liver with some bacon he had in his pack, settled the animals for the night and laid down with a full belly for his second night in the lonely cabin. It was December 22.

Running Doe pressed the canteen to her husband's fevered lips and felt his head. He was hot. The fever was taking him. She pulled the buffalo robe tighter around him, took the horse's lead and began again. The snow was deeper now and still falling. She could feel the child inside her stir and kick. Perhaps he would be a strong warrior like his father. She thought of her child as a man-child. She knew it was in the hands of the Father of skies, but still she wanted a man child. The thought kept her warm in the midst of this wearying cold. She trudged on.

She was wrapped in a blanket she had traded for back at Ft. Pierce and another buffalo robe her father had given her when she was married. There was no food, but she would do something. Her father had taught her well before they were forced to live at Standing Rock Reservation. She would find food. With the snow there would always be water. She walked on leading the horse, dragging her fevered wounded husband on the travois. Their tracks were quickly being covered by the falling snow. That was a good thing. She knew the soldiers were after them. How foolish to believe the Ghost Dancers.

How foolish to believe a white shirt would stop a bullet. Her husband had been one of the men guarding Sitting Bull when the reservation police came to arrest him. She grimaced as her unborn child kicked in her womb as the memory of her husband stumbling into their cabin his blood staining the white leather dark. She knew what had happened. She knew she had to escape. She packed to travel, rebandaged her husband's wound, wrapped him in the buffalo robe and in the darkness made her stealthy way out of the reservation across the plains.

That was many days ago. She didn't know how many but her steps had brought her many miles. Walk. Stop to rest. Care for her husband. Sleep wherever the weariness took her. Rise. Walk. Stop. Over and over walk, rest, walk, stop. She had seen no one. She did not want to see anyone. She had crossed the Dakotas alone.

Christmas Time

People meant news of them. News of them meant soldiers. She walked on. The night came quickly in late December. They came to a stream with a rime of ice around the edges of the stones. She knew if she got wet she might freeze. She picked her way carefully across stepping on the stones, praying the pinto would not stumble, that the travois would hold together. They made it safely to the other side. She drew the pony into the firs. Unhitched the sledge and pulled it and her husband under the shelter of the massive spruce. It was like a small tepee. The cover of needles underneath was soft and the tree held its warmth. She settled the pinto hoping he would find something to eat.

She made her way quietly down to the stream. In the soft reflection of the fading light she could see the shadows of the trout coasting in the current. She pulled back her sleeve and eased her ungainly form down the water's edge. Slowly she put her hand into the icy water. The cold felt like fire running up her arm. She moved her hand ever so little and stopped. Then again a little and stillness. Gradually she was at the fish. It was a big one from what she could see in the gloom. Enough for both of them. For three of them for there was the living child inside her to feed as well. She eased her hand in place and with a single motion she swept the fish under the gills and onto the bank. She hit it with a stone to stop its thrashing. She could not start a fire because of the smoke.

She cleaned the fish with her knife and stripped its flesh from its bones and fed herself, her child and her wounded husband. She washed her hands in the stream; crawled in beside her husband to share his warmth, give him hers and slept. She woke to the sound of bits and bridles, horses shod with iron. Through the branches of the tree she could see the soldiers on the other side of the stream.

"What do you see, Walking Hand?" Said the Lieutenant. "Any sign of them?" "There is nothing, Lieutenant." There was something if only the foolish white man could read the signs, but he could not. Walking Hand would not give this woman away. She was only saving her man and child from death. He had heard the stories of the arrest of Sitting Bull.

He knew the white man's fears, but he knew the Lakota's fears too. Sitting Bull had been shot in the side and the head when the Lakota police had come to take him. An Indian shot by Indians. There was a struggle. Shots were fired. People died. He had tracked her for many miles, but this was far enough. He knew the soldiers would not want to cross the water in the cold. He smiled at their weakness. "There is nothing. We have lost her in the snow. She will die soon anyway because of the cold. We will not join her." Slowly the column turned around churning the snow and any signs others might read later. They headed back toward the fort and the warmth of the barracks.

The silence flooded in again. As Running Doe watched them turn, she knew the scout had seen the signs. She saw him search the far edges of the stream. She knew he saw her. He smiled. She could not hear his words, but she saw the horse soldiers go. She knew they would not search for her again. She crawled back beside her husband and slept. She awoke when her husband spoke in his fevered sleep. She scooped snow into her mouth. Pressed some to his lips, hitched the travois and began to lead the pinto once again. The snow was deeper still and the going was hard. She knew she had crossed the trail of the cows. It reached many miles from the south. She only hoped that with the driving snow they would not be seen in the open flatland.

She knew too of the quicksand, the alkali flats and the other dangers. All day she headed west with the north wind pressing against her as she tried to hide on the shoulder of the pinto. It pulled at her. It wrapped around her husband under the buffalo robe and worked to sink its fingers into her heart. She began to chant softly for Sitting Bull and the other braves who had died at Standing Rock. Her voice snatched away by the wind and falling snow. The early darkness closed about them as they came to the woods of the Wyoming territory. Each step seemed heavier than the last. Even the pony was having trouble in the deep snow. The branches of the firs around her barely stirred.

There was only silver silence of the falling snow, the slightest whisper of snow on snow sifting gently down through the trees and branches of the darkening woods. The baby kicked and she gasped in pain and surprise. Then she smelled it, the smoke and the scent of meat cooking. The pony nickered in recognition of others of his kind somewhere ahead. She could feel him quicken, his head held high, looking, searching. Her mouth began to water as the scent drew nearer winding its way in and around the forest through which she trudged. What should she do? Who was in the cabin? She crept closer, as silent as the wind in her swollen form. At that moment her husband cried out in Lakota and the pony neighed loudly. In a flash the cabin door flew open and a faint light spilled out into the night. In the doorway was a man with a rifle pointed at her. The baby kicked and her body collapsed as the contractions hit her. She cried out as she fell. Jesse put the rifle back in the cabin and sped forward toward the kneeling squaw. He gathered her up and bore her to the shack. He laid her gently on the pallet he had prepared for himself. "My husband." Running Doe whispered. Jesse went back out and found the fevered man on the travois. He peeled back the robes and saw the blood. Even in the cold he could smell the wound suppurating. In a moment Jesse had the man inside laid out on the floor near the small fire he had going. "Help us, please." Said the woman.

Jesse put more wood on the fire and stirred the blaze. He knelt beside the man and began to uncover the wound. "The bullet is still inside him?" He questioned. She nodded.

A thousand thoughts raced through his mind, but there was no time for them now. He knew what needed to be done. He had seen it a hundred times in the war. He had done it a few times himself over the years. Gently he probed the wound with his hand. The man groaned a deep guttural moan. Jesse grabbed the bottle of whiskey he kept with him and slowly poured it over the wound. He heard the man gasp as the alcohol hit the bullet hole in his side. Jesse sloshed some over his hands and his knife before holding it over the fire. Slowly and gently he slid the blade into the wound. There was a slight hiss of the hot knife on flesh. A shudder ran through the brave as the blade went in. Jesse felt the hardness of the bullet through the handle of the knife. Now he knew where it was. "This is going to hurt, but the bullet must come out."

He pushed down hard with one hand around the wound while he sank his fingers in to the wound. He could feel the lead with his fingertips. He pushed harder until he could grasp the metal with his fingers. He pulled it out, his hand covered in blood. He poured more whiskey in the wound. Then he grabbed the .44 shells from his case and pried out the lead with his knife. "Three should be enough." He said to himself.

He shook out the powder from the shells onto the wound, took a flaming branch from the fire and ignited the powder. He covered his eyes as it flashed brightly. The powder burned. The woman screamed and the man cried out and then lost consciousness. It was done. Jesse cleaned and dressed the wound, packing it tightly as he wrapped the clean rags he always carried around the body. Except for her cry Running Doe had watched silently as the stranger went through all this. He seemed to know what to do and she was too weak to stop him. When all was done the man stepped outside to wash his hands in the snow. He crouched by the fire to warm them when he returned. He held out his canteen to her. Running Doe took it and drank the water in one long slow pull. Jesse cut off some of the elk he had been cooking and gave it to her. She ate slowly, her fatigue dragging at her limbs. She looked at her husband and then back at Jesse. "He'll sleep now for a while. Your man will wake when the fever breaks. We'll see what the wound does. Do you understand me?" Running Doe nodded wearily, turned on her side and went to sleep.

Jesse pulled her blanket over her and tended the fire. He went out and settled the pinto. Threw down more fodder for the hungry beast and wondered what to do next.

This was not in his plan, but then he had no plan except to ride the trail and check on the railway holdings.

He did not want to start caring for these people. He had not cared for anyone or anything since he lost his family. He leaned the travois against the shack and eased himself back into the warm room. He tried to stay awake with his back to the wall, but his eyes closed and sleep overtook him. He came to, checked on his two guests and faded back into oblivion. He woke to the smell of coffee. Slowly he opened his eyes and saw the woman beside the fire with the pot in her hand. She poured a cup and handed it to him. He smiled and reached for the handle. He nodded his thanks and let the liquid warm him. Whatever else she did she could make coffee. "Thank you for your help." She said plainly. "You have been very kind." "My pleasure, ma'am. If you don't mind my asking, what happened?" "You have heard of Sitting Bull?" "Oh yes. Who hasn't? I saw him a while back in one of Buffalo Bill Wild West Shows. He rode around on his horse and cursed the people in Lakota. I don't think they knew what he was saying." "Yes," She smiled. "He told me about that one afternoon while I was waiting for my husband. My husband was one of his guardians. ""Guards, ma'am?" "No, my husband protected him." "Yes, I see. Is that how your man was shot?"
"Yes, the Lakota police came for Sitting Bull. Shots were fired. Sitting Bull was killed. My husband and others were wounded. I escaped with him before more trouble came." "You walked all the way from Standing Rock? In this?"

"Yes, it was all there was to do." "I'm Jesse, Jesse Cox." "I am called Running Doe." "Looks like you're about to drop a faun, ma'am." Running Doe smiled at the words. It had been long since she smiled. "Only the deer does not birth in the winter, does she?" "No ma'am got more sense than that." "He will come soon, this man child." "Just in time for Christmas." Jesse said. "Yes, just like the baby Jesus, born in a stable." "You know about Jesus, ma'am?" "Yes, Mr. Jesse. The white missionary on the reservation spoke of Him, of the man with dark skin from a tribe who came to save us. I know of the story. I am a follower of the Father of skies. I am as you would say, a Christian. What of you, Mr. Jesse?" His eyes fell for a moment. "I don't believe in much, ma'am. I've seen too much evil to believe there's any good in the world." "There is always good, Mr. Jesse. What you have done for us is good. Helping my husband is good. The missionary is good. He helped us and brought the good news about Jesus. This baby is good." She smiled as she rubbed her swollen belly. Jesse did not know what to say to that so he kept his silence. He leaned over and felt for heat in the man's head. "His name is Weeping Fox." She said. "His fever has broken. If he will keep sleeping he will heal, ma'am." "That is good. I was. . . I was afraid for him. He was a Ghost Dancer.
He believed with others that the white leather shirt would turn a bullet.

Even though what was taught in the beginning was good, my people turned the good into a story to defeat the white man. We just want to live our lives." "Yes, ma'am. I guess that's what everyone wants."

The silence fell between them each wrapped in the truth of these words and what it had brought into the world. "I best see to the animals, Ma'am. I'll be right back." She nodded her assent and he left. "You just stop it, Jesse Cox. You just stop caring about these people. Caring about people brings nothing but trouble. Trouble and hurt. You've had enough of both for a lifetime." He whispered these words to himself as he lay down fodder for the animals and cleaned up around them as best he could. The snow had continued to fall through the night wrapping everything in its whiteness. He lowered the elk meat and cut some for their breakfast. He didn't think he could look cold jerky in the face this morning. He shook and stamped to rid himself of the snow before he went into the cabin. Running Doe was changing the dressing on her husband's wound. Already it was less inflamed and smelled better. She had heated some water and was washing his face and chest. Weeping Fox stirred a little as her hands passed over him. "Water" he whispered. These were the first coherent words he had spoken in over a week. Quickly she lifted his head slightly and pressed the canteen to his lips. He swallowed.

A smile passed over his face and he sank back into a deep sleep; his breathing deep and regular. Running Doe finished bathing him and covered her husband again with the robe. Jesse returned. "How is he, ma'am?" She was smiling. "He asked for water. Just the one word, but the only one with sense he has spoken for many days now." "That's good. Maybe he is going to make it. Have you thought about what you will do? Where you will go?" "The baby will come soon, I think. After that we will keep heading west until we can go no further. I have heard of a town called Frisco. It is large. Perhaps large enough for us to hide." "It's plenty large, Ma'am. It's called San Francisco and it is large. I was there once awhile back. Lots of Chinese there and Mexicans, but not so many Indians." "Are there other places, large places where we could hide?" "It's a big country and on West there are big cities with lots of people, but is that what you really want?" "I do not want my child to know the fear of the White man. I do not want my child to know the poverty of the reservation. I do not want my child to live as we have lived. Is this so much to want, Mr. Jesse? Do you have children, Mr. Jesse? A wife?" "I did once, ma'am, long ago. They were killed, murdered, in the Civil War. You know of this war?" "Yes, I learned of it at the mission school. General Custer fought in this war, yes?" "Yes, the fool. He had no business doing what he did, getting all his men killed. He was after the glory." "You do not think him a hero?"

Christmas Time

"From what I heard, he disobeyed orders. He took a few hundred soldiers against several thousand Indians. His arrogance got him in a battle he should never have fought. It was over in less than an hour with his men scattered dead over half a mile. The Lakota, your people ma'am, were just defending themselves." "You are very different from the white men I have met, Mr. Jesse." "Is that a good thing, ma'am?" "Yes, Mr. Jesse it is a good thing... Mr. Jesse, can you, would you, tell me of your wife?" "That was a long time ago, Running Doe. I do not speak of it. It changed me, wounded me." "Perhaps, Mr. Jesse it is like the wound of my husband. The bullet must be removed before the wound will heal. Like the bullet you took from my husband it is harming you." "Ma'am, if I may say so, you are not like any Indian woman I have ever met." "Have you met many?" "Just you, ma'am…." Jesse took a deep breath and thought of what she had said. He began to speak of Rachel. He could see her in his mind's eye as clearly as the last day he saw her. "She had long brown hair and brown eyes. When she smiled her whole face would light up. It was like she had a light inside her that would spill out when she smiled. Rachel was filled with sweetness. The only time I ever saw her get mad was once when she saw a man kick a cat that was brushing up against him. She marched right up to him even though he was much taller and bigger and just got in his face with her finger.

She asked him what the cat had ever done to him and what if someone kicked him if he got in their way and who did he think he was anyway. I laughed to see it. I laugh now. We had known each other since we were little. I had fancied her for years before I got up the courage to ask if I could court her. I had to ask her Pa and so we started courting sitting on her front porch with her Ma and Pa listening from the front parlor. Some nights there wasn't much to hear but the crickets. We just sat there. I was too afraid to speak, worried I would say the wrong thing and her too nice to tell me to go. After a while I asked her Pa if we could get married. He said he thought she was too good for me and I said I thought so too. He laughed at that and told me to go ahead. Rachel said yes and we were married. We moved in with my folks for a bit because I was helping my father on our farm, but then he gave me a piece of land and we built a house ourselves and moved in. Life went along. I'll never forget the day she told me she was pregnant with Jacob. She hadn't been to the doctor, but she knew. Then Jacob was born and I was as proud as a peacock. I built him a cradle. I made him some toys. Life was good. Then the war came along. I joined up out of duty. I fought 'til the end. I got wounded a few days before General Lee surrendered and I ended up in a field hospital. All I wanted to do was go home and see my family. By the time I could get about there wasn't a horse to be had and no money.

I thought if I could just get home everything would be all right. I started walking. It took weeks. That's how I know what you've been through. By the time I got home it was too late. My Rachel was dead on the floor of our bedroom covered in flies. She had been . . . attacked, you know. " Running Doe nodded. "She had been attacked and when I went to look for Jacob I found him with his head smashed in. He was so little and helpless.
I buried them both out in a grove near the house. I found a confederate button and pieces of a uniform when I went back to search the place for any signs of what happened. The stragglers had stolen everything worth stealing and left their clothes. I caught up with them in the next town. One of them was wearing my best suit and was trying to sell a cameo I had bought for Rachel one Christmas. I followed them to where they were camping in the woods and I killed them all. I should have killed myself alongside of Rachel, but I was too big a coward to do that.
My parents were dead by then and the carpetbaggers had come in and taken all the farms for taxes so I just headed west. Running away. I've been running ever since. I see Rachel and Jacob in my dreams and the faces of the men I killed in my nightmares so maybe I'm not the nice man you think I am and that's why I don't have much time for God. If there's a God, why does He let bad things like that happen? What had my Rachel or my Jacob ever done to Him?"

By now the tears were flowing down his face disappearing in his beard. Running Doe was crying as well because she now understood the weight he carried. "Mr. Jesse, these are evil things. Evil things happen, not because the Father of skies is evil, but because of the evil within us." "But why my Rachel and my Jacob?" "I do not know, Mr. Jesse. These are hard questions. Questions that only the Father of Skies can answer. I know that sometimes He tells us why, but sometimes He does not. Do you know the story of Job in the Bible?"

"Yes. I know about old Job. He had a rough time of it. Had all those sores and a nagging wife." Running Doe smiled. "He lost his riches, his health and his children, but he would not curse God. In the end when the Father of skies appeared in the whirlwind the Father asked, 'Where were you when I made the earth?' This I know, Mr. Jesse, the Father is good and knows all things. I do not know why my man was shot. I do not know why the Father of skies drove me across the Dakotas. I do not know why my baby will be born here in the middle of the wilderness in the deep snow, but I know the Father of skies is with me. I know He holds me in His hand. Let the Father of skies hold you in His hand, Mr. Jesse. Let Him remove the bullet from your wound. " The silence fell between them and then Jesse stood and walked out of the cabin into the snowy night.

Running Doe lifted her hands and began chanting slowly to the Father of skies praying for her husband and this stranger, Jesse that God had brought into her life.

Jesse waded deep into the woods through the drifted snow. Hot tears were flowing down his cheeks cooling and frosting on his face and beard. He pulled his knife from his belt and placed the razor edge against his throat. His breath was coming in ragged sobs as his sorrow and anger overtook him.

He tensed his arm ready to draw the blade across his throat and spill his blood on the virgin snow to end his life, but he did not move. He stood there frozen in time with the blade growing cold against his skin, his chest slowly heaving with each labored breath blowing vapor clouds to fill the air. He shouted a deep guttural moan as he plunged the knife into the bark of the tree in front of him again and again releasing his anger and his sorrow. Jesse fell to his knees in the deep snow the cold wrapping him in its embrace. "Dear God, I been running from you a long time and I'm so tired. My mama and daddy knew you. My Rachel knew you. I've heard about you all my life. Forgive me. Forgive me for my anger, my hate. Forgive me for killing those men who killed my family. I don't know what to do about that. It's been a long time. I reckon You'll show me. Take me, God. Save me like the old chaplain talked about before the battles. That's all I know to say. Amen."

Suddenly he felt warmth surround him as Running Doe placed her buffalo robe about his shoulders. She had come up behind him silently in the snow. "Mr. Jesse, come now. Come with me out of the cold." He rose and allowed her to lead him back into the cabin feeling its warmth surround him as he entered and the warmth inside as his heart began to heal. "The bullet's out, Running Doe. The bullet's out. God just plunged his hand into my heart and pulled it right out just like I did for Weeping Fox. My fever's gone. I can start to heal." Her eyes turned to her husband as he continued to sleep the sleep that would bring him back to her. She turned back to Jesse. "This is good, Mr. Jesse. This is good. Now you can have Christmas in peace." "Running Doe, I forgot all about Christmas. It's tomorrow." Jesse went about the normal chores of caring for the animals. Spreading the fodder he had brought. He began to cast his mind about for what he could give his unexpected guests for Christmas now that it seemed he was going to celebrate it after all. Running Doe seemed fine, a burst of energy moving her to sweep out the cabin with her hands, clear out the cob webs and straighten anything that could be straightened. Jesse gathered wood, melted snow for water and dragged in branches and small cedars to give the animals a break against the wind and the cold. He cleared more snow away from the cabin.

Weeping Fox continued to sleep a deep healing sleep, coming to the surface just long enough to take a sip of water from the canteen Running Doe held to his lips. The winter's light began to fade, the cold bore down with the night. Jesse had made some sour dough from starter, baking it in the Dutch oven he always packed. A stew simmered in the fire made from elk, wizened carrots and potatoes from his stores. Running Doe and Jesse sat silently on the floor wrapped in their own thoughts while Weeping Fox continued to sleep. His soft deep breathing loud in the quiet. "Mr. Jesse, it is Christmas Eve. Would you like to read the Christmas story?" "Why sure, ma'am, but what will I read from. I mean, I know the story.

My mama used to tell us the story when we were small and I remember the preacher reading it from church, but I don't think I could get close to what the Bible says."

"I have a Bible, Mr. Jesse." Running Doe reached into a their bundle under the small bed and brought out a black cloth bound Bible , it's worn edges curled with use. She turned to the passage in Luke where the nativity story was recorded. "Here, Mr. Jesse, you read for us." Jesse took the Bible, tipped it toward the light of the fire and began to read. Slowly at first, because it had been a long time since he had read anything. Luke 2:"1 ¶ And it came to pass in those days, that there went out a decree from Caesar Augustus, that all the world should be taxed.

2 (And this taxing was first made when Cyrenius was governor of Syria.)3 And all went to be taxed, every one into his own city.4 And Joseph also went up from Galilee, out of the city of Nazareth, into Judaea, unto the city of David, which is called Bethlehem; (because he was of the house and lineage of David:)5 To be taxed with Mary his espoused wife, being great with child." Running Doe smiled a small smile and held her belly in her hands picturing the child within her. Jesse continued, " 6 And so it was, that, while they were there, the days were accomplished that she should be delivered." A short gasp came from Running Doe as a contraction came, short and sharp. "7 And she brought forth her firstborn son, and wrapped him in swaddling clothes, and laid him in a manger; because there was no room for them in the inn.8 ¶ And there were in the same country shepherds abiding in the field, keeping watch over their flock by night.
9 And, lo, the angel of the Lord came upon them, and the glory of the Lord shone round about them: and they were sore afraid.10 And the angel said unto them, Fear not: for, behold, I bring you good tidings of great joy, which shall be to all people.11 For unto you is born this day in the city of David a Saviour, which is Christ the Lord.12 And this shall be a sign unto you; Ye shall find the babe wrapped in swaddling clothes, lying in a manger. 13 And suddenly there was with the angel a multitude of the heavenly host praising God, and saying,14 Glory to God in the highest, and on earth peace, good will toward men.15 And it came to pass, as the angels were gone away from them into heaven, the shepherds said one to another, Let us now go even unto Bethlehem, and see this thing which is come to pass, which the Lord hath made known unto us.16 And they came with haste, and found Mary, and Joseph, and the babe lying in a manger.17 And when they had seen it, they made known abroad the saying which was told them concerning this child.18 And all they that heard it wondered at those things which

Christmas Time

were told them by the shepherds.19 But Mary kept all these things, and pondered them in her heart.20 And the shepherds returned, glorifying and praising God for all the things that they had heard and seen, as it was told unto them.21 ¶ And when eight days were accomplished for the circumcising of the child, his name was called JESUS, which was so named of the angel before he was conceived in the womb.22 And when the days of her purification according to the law of Moses were accomplished, they brought him to Jerusalem, to present him to the Lord;23 (As it is written in the law of the Lord, Every male that openeth the womb shall be called holy to the Lord;)24 And to offer a sacrifice according to that which is said in the law of the Lord, A pair of turtledoves, or two young pigeons.25 ¶ And, behold, there was a man in Jerusalem, whose name was Simeon; and the same man was just and devout, waiting for the consolation of Israel: and the Holy Ghost was upon him.26 And it was revealed unto him by the Holy Ghost, that he should not see death, before he had seen the Lord's Christ.27 And he came by the Spirit into the temple: and when the parents brought in the child Jesus, to do for him after the custom of the law,28 Then took he him up in his arms, and blessed God, and said,29 Lord, now lettest thou thy servant depart in peace, according to thy word:30 For mine eyes have seen thy salvation,31 Which thou hast prepared before the face of all people;
32 A light to lighten the Gentiles, and the glory of thy people Israel.33 And Joseph and his mother marvelled at those things which were spoken of him.34 And Simeon blessed them, and said unto Mary his mother, Behold, this child is set for the fall and rising again of many in Israel; and for a sign which shall be spoken against;35 (Yea, a sword shall pierce through thy own soul also,) that the thoughts of many hearts may be revealed. 36 And there was one Anna, a prophetess, the daughter of Phanuel, of the tribe of Aser: she was of a great age, and

had lived with an husband seven years from her virginity;37 And she was a widow of about fourscore and four years, which departed not from the temple, but served God with fastings and prayers night and day.38 And she coming in that instant gave thanks likewise unto the Lord, and spake of him to all them that looked for redemption in Jerusalem.39 And when they had performed all things according to the law of the Lord, they returned into Galilee, to their own city Nazareth.40 And the child grew, and waxed strong in spirit, filled with wisdom: and the grace of God was upon him."

Jesse finished reading and smiled. Weeping Fox turned slowly on his side and spoke, his voice weak and cracked. "Thank you, Mr. Jesse. It is good to wake and hear those words. I must have heard your name in my waking dreams. Thank you for your help. I am in your debt." "There are no debtors here, Weeping Fox." "How are you feeling?" "Better since you plunged your hand inside me to remove the bullet festering within, but I still am weak.

I think I could eat something if there is food." The aroma of the stew had filled the cabin and reminded them they were all hungry. "Will you say thanks, my husband?" "Father of Skies, we thank You for this which You have made. We thank You for making the elk to walk in the woods with his great size to feed many. We thank You for making the potatoes and carrots to grow in the earth which You also have made. I thank You for guiding us to this place to meet the one who could help us. Father of Skies we thank and worship You. Amen."

Running Doe ladled out the stew in the dented tin plates Jesse had given her. They ate in silence sopping up the gravy with the sour dough bread. They passed the canteen around each taking a long draw. "There is coffee." The aroma filled the hut mingling with the savory smell of the stew. "I'll have some of that, please. "Said Jesse.
"Water" Weeping Fox spoke weakly. Running Doe pressed the cup into Jesse's hands and helped her husband drink from the canteen. He was still very weak. "I could do with something sweet. How about you, Weeping Fox?" "Sweet?" "Yes, dessert." "What do you have, Mr. Jesse?"Spoke Running Doe. "Molasses, molasses on bread. Just the thing." Jesse reached deep into his pack and brought out a glass jar of dark sorghum molasses. He handed it to Running Doe who took some of the sour dough bread that was left, cut it in half and poured molasses onto the bread. She handed Jesse a dripping piece. He caught the excess on his finger and put it in his mouth.
Next she held a piece for her husband who took a small bite from her hand. The eating had used up what energy he had. A smile creased his face as the sweetness filled his mouth. "I like molasses. White man oppress Indian. White man keep molasses from Indian. Indian fight for molasses." Jesse's smile clouded as he held the bread to his lips. A look of hurt and worry crossed his face. "I tease you, Mr. Jesse.

Molasses is good. Thank you." The bread continued to Jesse's mouth and he smiled a sticky smile as Running Doe laughed at his discomfort. Suddenly Running Doe gasped and grabbed her belly. "The baby is coming now." She put her hand on the side of the shack and levered her way up. She rushed to the door holding her hand beneath her belly. Jesse started after her, but Weeping Fox called him back. "No. No let her go." "She'll freeze, the baby will freeze." "She must do this alone. It is our way. Leave her. With no women here she will have the baby on her own. It is our way. "

Running Doe stumbled through the drifts of snow. Even as she held her belly her eyes were searching for a place to have the child. There. There was a place. A small tree grew in a hollow of ground. As the contractions went through her she began to kick at the snow. Then she grabbed a fallen branch and swept a clear place. Next she began tearing at the branches of a fir tree and laying them on the place she had cleared. Stopping to let the pain wash through her and give a low guttural growl with each pain. Finally the place was ready to catch the baby.

She grabbed the tree, squatted and began to push with each contraction. The men could hear her groans and it was all Jesse could do to keep from going to her, helping her, but Weeping Fox, his face of stone, stopped him. "She will make a place to have the baby. She will use a tree or stick to help her.

The baby will drop to the ground. She will cut and tie the cord and clean the baby with the snow and then she will return." "But you just can't leave her to do this on her own." Jesse said. "She will do this. It is the way of the woman with child." They could hear the noises getting louder and louder as the contractions grew.

Finally there was a long low growl and then silence. A baby's cry broke the stillness and the men smiled. "I think we will call him Jesse Snow Elk." "Him?" "Running Doe thinks it is a boy." "I think we'll know soon enough." They could hear the soft cry of the new born and Running Doe's step through the snow. The shack door swung open and Running Doe stepped in with the baby in her arms. "You have a son. What will you call him." "I think he will be called Jesse Snow Elk for the two that have saved us. Jesse who sheltered us and the elk that fed us." "He will be called Jesse Snow Elk." Running Doe said. She sat by the fire and began softly crooning to the baby, slowly rocking back and forth. Jesse stood with his mouth open and his brows furrowed. "You just had a baby." "Yes, Jesse." "When a white woman has a baby she stays in the bed weak as water." "Jesse, I have just crossed the Dakotas with the baby and my husband. I am sitting by the fire. That is enough rest for me. It is our way, Jesse." Weeping Fox smiled at the strength of his wife and for his new born son. Jesse sat amazed at Running Doe.

Soon she began to nurse the baby covered by the blanket from the bed. Jesse could hear the soft suckling noise and the low coo the baby made as he ate. It brought back the feeling he had when Jacob was born and he rejoiced inside that God had brought joy and feeling back into his heart again. Weeping Fox had fallen asleep again and Running Doe closed her eyes resting with the baby in her arms. Jesse went out and checked on the animals again making sure all was as secure as it could be in the wilderness. He had decided what to give his guests, his friends for Christmas. He went through it in his mind as eager for Christmas morning now as he had been in many long years. He went back into the shack, wrapped himself in a buffalo robe and slept.

He heard the baby in the night and Running Doe caring for her child. He would come just to the edge of wakefulness and then slide back down into the peace of sleep. Jesse woke again to the aroma of coffee and bacon frying in a pan. He could also smell something baking. He opened his eyes to see almost every pan he possessed brought in to service for this breakfast. Weeping Fox was sitting upright with his hands wrapped around a cup of coffee. "Good, Jesse, you are awake. I thought I would have to shake you. Christmas morning breakfast is ready." Again Weeping Fox prayed and Running Doe served out coffee, bacon and hoe cake covered in elk gravy. Running Doe had made a place for the baby in a nest of buffalo robe and blanket.

Christmas Time

He was sleeping. They finished their meal each replete with the warm food. Jesse spoke. "Weeping Fox, Running Doe it is Christmas. I don't know if you know about the white man custom of Christmas, but it is giving presents." "Yes, we know this, "spoke Weeping Fox. We do not do this because on the reservation there was little to give, but we know this . . . tradition." "I have something for you. . . .for Christmas." Jesse reached into his pack and pulled out three bundles. "For you, Weeping Fox." He handed the first bundle to Weeping Fox. It was long and narrow, wrapped in doe skin. Weeping Fox pulled the bow of string leather wrapped around the package. He began to unroll it. As the last fold fell open there in his hand was a large hunting knife. It had a handle of bone. The blade burned with the image of the fire and the lantern. "I traded a fella for the blade a while back. It's a good blade, good steel, all the way from Germany he said. Anyway, I made the handle. Carved it myself for myself, but I want you to have it." Weeping Fox eyes glowed with the knife. "Never had I had such a knife. Thank you, Jesse." Jesse smiled. He handed the next small bundle to Running Doe. Her eyes looked down as she took the small gift from his hands, but a smile of pleasure and anticipation curled around her lips. She slowly began to unwrap this package. Running Doe gasped as she held the unwrapped package in her hand. It was Rachel's cameo.

"I cannot accept this, Mr. Jesse. It is too much. This belonged to your Rachel." "I think she would want you to have it. Please accept it and wear it with joy." Slowly she untied the beaded necklace from around her throat. She took the cameo and attached it to the middle of the beads she always wore. It fell almost hidden in the folds of her doeskin jerkin. Finally he gave her another package. It rattled as she took it and when she opened it she found that was what it was. It was a carved bone rattle for the baby. "It was Jacob's. I carved it for him before he was born. I have carried it with me for many years now. Please, I want you to have it for your baby." "Thank you, Jesse, I know what this must mean to you. Thank you." "There is one more thing I would like to give you. I have a ranch. It is not big as ranches go, but it has a cabin and land and a barn. I would like for you to come live with me. It is out of the way. It will be a safe place to raise your family. We will build a place for you as soon as winter is over. I am gone a fair bit and it would be a great help to me to have someone there all the time. There is hunting and fishing for you Weeping Fox, as well as the cattle to care for to feed the railway workers. It is a good place. What do you say? It is much closer than Frisco. " Weeping Fox looked at Running Doe. She nodded and smiled. "We will come, Mr. Jesse. You have rescue us from the cold and from harm. Thank you." " No, Weeping Fox. It is you who have rescued me."

3 DOC TAYLOR

Old Doc Taylor made his weary way home. He was tired. Two broken arms, one wicked gash from a skittish mare and a case of the mumps. He smiled as the old Christmas song resolved itself in his head. "Five young with measles, four broken elbows, three cracked ribs, two pulled muscles and a patella with lacerations." The tune flowed silently in his head. "When you can still laugh at trouble, things can't be too bad." He spoke the words aloud, though; there was no one to hear but old Max. Max had taken Doc Taylor on many a call. He'd pulled the buggy through heat and swollen rivers, through biting cold and blossoming spring. Now it was Christmas, their twelfth Christmas together, Doc's Fortieth as a country physician. The snow was falling, not silently, but with the soft whisper that made you think of new washed sheets snapped out and floating to the bed below. Bed, he hadn't seen that since three o'clock this morning and now it was nearly ten at night. He could see the lights of home shining off the fallen snow. It always made him think of heaven on nights like tonight. Home, shining like Heaven, all golden and warm and welcoming him in. Home where there was love and rest.

Yes, his home was a lot like heaven. Jesus lived there. Christ was the head of his home. Elspeth would be there too with supper ready and coffee hot. It never seemed to matter what time he got home, she always had things ready. She'd learned long ago about being a doctor's wife. She knew he tried his best to make it home in time or let her know when he'd be in, but after all these years she understood. She never complained, though in the early years there'd been a lot of silent tears, burned roasts and biscuits that would fell a bull.

Long years filled with love, with family, three children, all doctors, NOT in the country, long years in which the lives of an entire county wove in and around and through his memory, like the vine wreathing the Taylor front door. All this ran through his mind while he settled Max for the night, made his way to the house, eased out of his old coat, kissed Elspeth and sat down to his dinner.

"How was your day, Love, asked Elspeth? She always asked, always listened as she did tonight, listened through every illness, every accident, every birth, every death. Deaths were hardest, but still she listened and loved. "You work too hard!" she always said that. His reply was always the same, "I don't know how to work soft.

I suppose I could have told the Matthews boy with the broken arm I was too tired, I'll come back next week sometime after I've rested." "You need a vacation," Elspeth went on.

Christmas Time

"All right, we'll go to Paris come spring. "Doc teased. "No, we didn't go to Paris last year", she replied. "Well, the Riviera then," Doc responded. "No, we didn't go there the year before and the year before that we didn't take a cruise around the world. So don't tell me we'll do that either. I know you, we'd be arm in arm looking at the moon over the Atlantic and you'd remember Alistair Pembine's lumbago." "Alistair Pembine does not have lumbago; he has persistent idiopathic imagination and a terminal case at that. One of these days he'll imagine himself to death, but what he really is, is lonely." "And he lets you beat him at checkers if you and Max go out to his place," was Elspeth's perceptive response. They had said it all before one way or another. They had teased this way for nearly forty years, always the same, always with love, always content. This year was going to be different he thought to himself. Christmas was two days away and this year she was going to be surprised. Patients who had owed him money for years had suddenly taken a notion to pay him, must have been the new preacher down the valley, he thought wryly, but they had paid whatever the reason. This year under the tree Fred Arnold brought by to pay for his ear infection, there were going to be two tickets, two round trip tickets on a steamer to England and then on to Paris.

If only the babies would wait and the old folks could hang on just a little bit longer, this Christmas would be just about perfect. The twenty-third passed with nothing more than the usual sniffles, coughs, scratches, and sprains that came with winter. No one wanted to be laid up over Christmas. "Saving it up for the day after," his nurse had said. Nurse Shaw had come to him shortly after taking over the practice. He was never quite sure whether he'd hired her or the other way around, but she was the perfect nurse for a country practice. Although she'd always managed to convey with the entrance of every patient it would be a miracle if this one didn't die before the end of the visit. Doc Taylor hadn't ever gotten over the feeling that she thought somehow she knew more than any doctor who ever lived, with the exception of Luke, and she didn't understand why more of his patients didn't end up at the cemetery sooner. She was more than likely right about saving it up though. It always seemed to happen that way.

Christmas Eve dawned gray and cold with the promise of snow. The Farmer's Almanac had said so and it was nearly always right. A few patients straggled in. Everybody was trying to get ready for Christmas. He did treat a wonderfully set of singed eyebrows on Mr. Powell. Peeking in at the Christmas goose, served ***him*** right his wife had said, stay out of ***her*** kitchen next time. Hard to keep a straight face during that one. Noon came with no one in the waiting room.

Christmas Time

He decided they'd close up and go home early. Everyone in the valley knew where the Doc lived so if there was any real trouble they knew where to find him. He sent Nurse Shaw off with a Merry Christmas, hitched up Max and made his way home. In the back of his mind was Mrs. Kennedy. He'd been to check on her just yesterday. He thought she'd wait a few more days to have that baby, but he wasn't sure. "You can never tell with babies, they come when they please" he spoke aloud to Max who nodded apparently thinking of all the late nights he'd had as well. At home, Christmas preparations were in full swing. The house was filled with smells of Christmas. Elspeth had put some of the apple wood logs on the fire. Bread was baking, pies were cooling. Cider was mulling. Christmas had arrived at the Taylor home.

The children and grandchildren would be there for dinner Christmas Day and there would be presents and laughter and memories of other Christmases filling the house. Tonight he would surprise Elspeth like he hadn't surprised her since he asked her to marry him. His eyes lit up with the very thought of it. This Christmas was going to be one of the all-time best.

Dinner was over, the baking done for the night, the tempest in abeyance, temporarily. It would all start again Christmas morning. Doc and Elspeth were together in the old settee. She was knitting a final set of mittens for one of the grandchildren.

Usually he would be napping and tending to the fire, but he wasn't napping tonight. He was waiting, savoring each splendid moment until he would give Elspeth her present.

It was now nearly ten, the snow had begun in earnest. The wind drove the snow to the ground. Inside by the fire was a good place to be. Doc was at home surrounded by everything he loved. Contentment. He was content. Contentment vanished in a moment with the pounding at the door. He rushed to reach it, hoping, but the knock at the door had happened too often in his life for him not to expect the worst. It was Amy Kennedy. "Doctor, the baby's coming and Mama's having a real hard time. Daddy didn't want to leave her so I came," she finished half out of breath. She was shaking with cold and nearly spent. The Kennedy farm was a long way from the Doctor's. She had struggled through the deep snow alone. "I'll hitch up Max to the sleigh, you stay here with Elspeth. She'll take good care of you," Taylor threw the words over his shoulder as he moved toward the barn. "Is Momma going to be all right," Amy whispered. "I think so, child. I'll do my best. God will look out for her." And he was gone. Max was soon wading through heavy snow. It was bad, worse than the Doctor had ever faced. The snow beat down like tiny arrows. The cold was so fierce it bit right through his clothes. Even his old green sweater which had seen so many deliveries, so many cold nights, couldn't keep him warm tonight.

Christmas Time

Max was a blackness in the white storm. A light would appear through the night; occasionally a fence post would loom out of the darkness to show Taylor he was still on his way to Kennedy's farm. Taylor and Max were just below the Kendall farm when the worst occurred. The sleigh stopped. Doc Taylor slapped up Max with the reins but he didn't move. The Doctor slowly climbed down, following the reins. Max was down.

Doc Taylor followed the lines of the great dark body to Max's head. Taylor pulled with all his might at the harness. It was no use. Max wouldn't move. His breathing was labored, the eyes glassy. "Max, good boy, good Max, easy boy. It's all right. Quietly Max's head drooped, breathing stopped. He was gone. There was no time to be sorry, no time to miss his companion of many years. There was still a baby to deliver, a life to save, lives to save. Taylor slowly tried to pierce the driving snow. Yes, yes, there were the lights of the Kendall place. Of all places to look for refuge. Thomas Kendall was the most cantankerous coot in the whole valley.

"How his wife put up with him all these years is beyond me," Elspeth had puffed one Sunday after church. Kendall was the best and richest farmer around, but a hard man. It was as if his crops grew out of a dread of his displeasure. Everything was orderly. Buildings whitewashed. Large herds. He came to church every Sunday wearing the same bow tie for the last thirty years. Elspeth had commented on that as well.

"Too cheap by half." All this washed over Taylor as he labored up the drive to the farmhouse.

He wasn't sure Kendall would help. "Lord, give me strength. Watch over that mother and her coming child," prayed Taylor as he climbed the steps.

He beat desperately on the door. Jean Kendall answered. "Doc? Doc? Come in! What's wrong?" "Horse died, got to get to Kennedy's, baby coming," he gasped. "I'll get Thomas," spoke Jean. Seconds passed as the snow began to puddle at Taylor's feet in the hall. Thomas Kendall entered in a huff. "You want me to go out on a night like this to take you to deliver a baby? And for that, that Kennedy? He's never done anything for me, why should I help him. He probably can't even pay you. Babies have come without doctors before this," Kendall growled. "None of **your** babies ever came without a doctor," his wife pressed. "I suppose people will talk about me if I don't take you. Get to the barn. I'll hitch up the sledge," Kendall replied with ill grace. "Don't know why a baby would want to come on a night like this anyway."

Soon Taylor and Kendall were struggling through the cold to the Kennedy farm, Kendall muttering all the way. The going was hard and the Doctor had many agonizing moments thinking of the Kennedys. Finally they reached the old farm. Richard Kennedy rushed through the driving snow to meet them.

He hurried the Doctor inside while Kendall put the horses away in a barn he wouldn't keep his pigs in.

A woman's cry pierced the storm as Kendall made his way up the back steps to the house. Thomas Kendall thought he had stepped into bedlam. Several small children were on the floor in the kitchen, all were crying. Water was boiling violently on the stove and what looked like the beginnings of Christmas dinner were here and there in stages of disaster. The Doctor rushed into this scene to place his instruments in the boiling water. "I'll just wait in the parlor, Doctor," spoke Kendall. "You'll do no such thing. You'll look out for these children," Taylor ordered. "What? I'm not taking care of any passel of children," Kendall shouted over the crying. Taylor was fierce, "Look, you can take care of the children or you can help me with this birth.

Choose one or the other, but there's no waiting in the parlor tonight." Kendall looked like he'd been asked to choose between a toothache and broken leg. He breathed deeply and spoke in a resigned whisper, "Give me the children." "What?" Taylor spoke. "I said, 'give me the children,'" Kendall replied hoarsely. The Doctor returned to his patient with a determined smile. Kendall faced the children, all girls, all under age six. A low growl came from deep inside Kendall. That got their attention. He dried their tears, wiped their noses and silenced their cries with the same efficiency he used on his farm.

He herded them into the parlor like a bunch of unruly calves and sat them all down. Silence filled the small room. Then the six year old began to sniffle quietly, tears flowing down her soft cheeks. The two year old stared; the four year old clung to a ragged doll and sucked her thumb. Slowly the two year old crossed to Kendall, held up her arms and said, "Hold me." Kendall looked as if someone had put a frog in his coffee. "Hold me," the little one repeated.

Kendall picked up the child and placed her on his knee. He had become so stiff he looked as if he might break. "Story," whispered the two-year old. "What?" "The (She) wanths you to tell uth a thory," the six-year old lisped through missing front teeth. "You just be quiet, sit still and stop crying. I don't like crying." Kendall barked. The tears flowed anew. "Story" repeated the two-year old Anna. "I don't know any stories, especially stories for little girls," Kendall sulked. "Tell uth the thory about the baby," lisped Alice. "I don't know any stories about babies, little girl," said Kendall. "My namth Alith, this ith Anna, and thath Adele, all our namth begin with A," spoke Alice as she too climbed into Kendall's lap. Then Adele made her way across the parlor, doll in hand and climbed into Kendall's lap crowding her sisters. "The thory about baby Jethuth. My Momma telth uth that thory a lot. Don't you know that thory? I know that thory, let me tell you."

Slowly with her childish lisp and childlike faith Alice began to tell Thomas Kendall the story of the Christ Child in a way he'd never heard before. The angels, the shepherds, the stable, the manger, the Savior. Tonight, for the first time he was hearing it with his heart and the truth of its message touched him deep in his soul. Thomas Kendall was born anew.

Reborn on the same night we celebrate the coming to earth of the good news, the Christ Child, to spread the Gospel as this small child had told it tonight.

There was another birth that night, Angela Noel Kennedy was welcomed into the world by an old doctor who had brought hundreds of children into it, but who never failed to be in awe of the beauty of life and the miracle of birth. Richard Kennedy held his newest daughter in his arms with all the love he had for the others as he showed her off to her sisters and placed her in the arms of Thomas Kendall. "Thank you for giving her to us tonight. If you hadn't helped the Doc she never would have joined us," beamed Kennedy. With a choking voice Kendall spoke, "Your family has given me something as well. This has been a night of births. Thank you, thank you for my soul." As the meaning of Kendall's words sank into the hearts of the two men the sun rose over Christmas Day. Taylor and Kendall made their way slowly to the Doctor's house where Kendall settled Kennedy's account and promised the Doctor a new horse.

Taylor shook hands and thanked him with a smile. He invited Kendall in, but Mr. Kendall said he had a gift of his own to share and the sledge pulled away. Dr. Taylor slipped into the house. Elspeth was asleep in the settee. He woke her gently with tickets in his hand and shared with her what was indeed the best Christmas ever.

The End

4 CHRISTMAS LIGHT 1905

White flakes of snow swirled, floated, soared and faded into the gray ocean as the winds whirled around the lighthouse. The sea crashed relentlessly on the rocks that wrapped the light; each passing breaker flowing around it in its isolation. Adam's gaze swept the sea from left to right as he stood leaning against the wrought iron railing surrounding the top of the lighthouse where the granite blocks melded with the sheltering glass. He could hear the answering roar as the waves reached the shoals and reefs that dotted this expanse. It was his tiny fiefdom. He was its king. He was its sole inhabitant. His father had banished him to this wasteland to see what life was all about. How was he supposed to learn about life when there was none? There was only this gray-green sea stretching endlessly out before him. He had pumped up the oil for the lamp. He had sloshed water on the glass protecting the lens. He had polished the reflector. He had cleaned the lens with vinegar.

He had done all the chores on the list left by the keeper bribed by his father to let his son have a little privacy to think about things. No doubt that hoary old geezer was enjoying himself on the mainland in Newport in the warm comfort of a pub. "And what is life all about anyway?" He said softly to himself. "You were born, you lived life in the way that suited you and you died. End of story." If you were rich you lived well and comfortably and if you were poor you struggled and that was that.

His life to this point growing up as one of the Five Hundred on the Social Register with summers in Newport and winters in St. Simon, boarding schools, summer camp, Yale and all that went with that had been singularly pleasantly uneventful. He saw no reason to change for all that his father wanted him to "think about things." What a dreary phrase that was! What bore thinking about? He had a good life and he was bent on keeping it. Adam pounded the railing for emphasis and turned to climb through the trap door into the lighthouse.

Each day of his exile out of boredom Adam had rowed the tiny skiff to the small tide bound rocks that broke the surface of the sea around the light. The very rocks the light was supposed to warn against. Each day he had wandered the rocks finding the flotsam and jetsam the sea had tossed up. He found beauty and ugliness; shells like bright jewels, half eaten carcasses of some unfortunate seagull.

He remembered his childhood on the shores at St. Simon. He and his family set up in tents with wooden floors like archeologists on a dig. They even had native bearers except these wore starched white jackets and black trousers and said "Yes, madam" and "no, sir" to his parents and "yes, young sir" to him. Those were golden days when he walked the shore with a bucket and spade and his world was young. A wave smacked the bow and brought him back to the present.

He enjoyed these ramblings. He enjoyed the childish pleasure of the seeking and finding of these tiny treasures. He confessed to himself he looked forward to the fossiking about on the sea swept rocks. Today the bow scraped on the first hummock of rock jutting from the sea. He jumped out and tethered the painter around a stone, his gum boots shining from the wet. His nose caught the passing smells of the sea, fish, salt, the iron smell from the rock as the wind whipped around him. Here he found a mermaid's purse, a rope of egg casings from a horseshoe crab, scallop shells and the inevitable oyster shells emptied by the gulls. As he wandered his eyes lit on an old umbrella frame its covering long since ripped away, but the carved ivory handle proclaimed it as a rich man's bauble.

He picked it up looking at the fine working of a crocodile head with scales curving to a crocodilian smile chased with gold and at the end, the eyes looked like rubies.

Pieces of driftwood cast haphazardly about the pitted stones. Everything told a story of its own; a dock wrecked, a tree uprooted, a ship battered, a life lost. He saw all this as a crab scurried away on articulated legs dragging a sliver of dead fish in its claw trying to beat the incoming wave. Here was an old shoe. There a cork buoy from a lobster trap, its blue and yellow markings scarred and scraped by the sea. As he walked the length of the small outcropping, his eyes cast downward searching for anything. His pace was random, wandering. A thundering boom from an outlying fist of stone caused him to look up. The sea was getting higher. He should get to the lighthouse before it got too rough to row back. As he turned he saw what he had thought was a large boulder and realized it was a trunk.

"This is more like it." He said aloud. He clambered toward it. "I'll put it in the boat and open it in comfort at the lighthouse." He spoke again aloud. "I'm talking aloud to myself and I've only been here a few days. Oh well, Father always said people who talk to themselves were talking to the wisest person in the room." He smiled at the recollection and the thought. The trunk was a good one, a bit scarred from the pounding sea.

Leather handles and brass fittings. Covered over with what had once been bisque canvas, a Vuitton steamer trunk. As he pondered the meaning of this he absently looked around.

There at the edge of the water was a form, a body. He dropped everything in his hands and ran to the water's edge. A young woman lay on her side, her face white against the dark rocks, a watery rivulet of blood from an abrasion on her forehead. She was breathing, slowly. He knelt beside her and felt her pulse. It was faint, but steady. As he gathered her in his arms she stiffened, came too for a moment and again went limp. Her wet clothing wrapped around a very pregnant belly. Her flaxen hair streamed like sea weed over her face and neck. Carrying a pregnant woman sheathed in a long wet skirt and sodden jacket is no easy feat, but he managed to get her back to the skiff. He went back to the trunk and wrestled it into the boat. He gathered the other things he had found, pushed off the rocks and rowed back to the lighthouse. The sea was rising and the gentle snow had turned into a maelstrom. He would need the light to guide him back.

Adam struggled the final few yards to ease the boat to the landing without crashing into the pilings. The swells had risen in these last few yards. Adam made fast to the bollards and began the difficult task of emptying the boat. He got the woman into the lighthouse. He made a pallet by the fire on the second floor.

He drew a blanket over her and ferried the rest of his finds up the narrow stairs into the main room. He dragged the skiff up as high as he could and tied it against the stone blocks by iron rings driven into the wall.

By the time he was finished the sea was crashing around the door. Before long it the swells would cover the door in their passing. Up until now he had been acting automatically, without thought; going through the motions. He had been doing just what needed to be done. Fatigue swept over him. He realized he was cold and wet. His teeth were chattering and his hands were shaking, his lips blue from cold. He went up the stairs two at a time and changed in his room in front of the coal grate. When he was warm and reasonably dry he went back down to see to the sleeping woman. She was beginning to moan and speak softly in a language he did not understand, but thought was Russian. Her eyelids began to flutter.

Adam pressed a little brandy to her lips and the color began to come back to her cheeks. "Spa`sibo, Thank you." She whispered. Adam pulled the woolen blanket up tighter around her and sat back on the floor. "Are you hungry? Do you want something to eat?" "Da. po`zhaluista Yes, please. Adam had put some tinned soup on the small coal stove to warm for his own mid-day meal. He took one of the chipped mugs left by the lighthouse keeper and poured the steaming broth into it. He carried it carefully to the woman and pressed it in her hands.

She sat up, leaning against the hearth. She bowed her head briefly and slowly began to drink the hot broth. Adam studied her surreptitiously as he drank his own chipped cup of broth.

"Where am I?" She asked after a few moments. "You are in a lighthouse. I found you washed up on one of the outlying rocks and brought you here. My name is Adam, Adam Dennett. Other than being cold, wet and imminently pregnant are you all right?" The ghost of a smile swept her lips. "Yes, I think so. I am called Anouyska Kilkhoff. Did you? Was there anyone else? . . Was I alone when you found me?" "Yes. Yes, you were the only pregnant woman washed up on the rocks today. Yesterday there were several and I'm sure there will be more tomorrow. This just seems to be where the pregnant women wash up. A constant stream of them lined up along the rocks." Again the slight curve of the corners of her lips but it faded as quickly as it appeared. Then her brow furrowed. "Were you expecting there to be someone else? Is there supposed to be someone else?" He questioned. The import of her questions suddenly becoming apparent to him. She was silent for a long time. Her eyes began to wander around the room. They rested on the ivory handled umbrella and her face became a mask. "That is my father's. We were traveling together on ship. There was wave. Enormous, gigantic. "Rogue wave" the sailors shout just before it break over ship. My father and I are taking turn on deck. Suddenly sailor cry out and ring bell. We thought was drill or action of ship. My father gasped aloud and hold me. When I looked up I see wave bigger than ever before I see. It engulfed the ship. We wash overboard.

I see my father go under. All our things were on deck. We are leaving ship. A private yacht was meeting us to take us to your New York for Christmas. I don't know what happened to the ship. My father was gone. The umbrella was his favorite. He have it with him on deck." "I'm sorry." Adam murmured. "He may be all right. He might have survived. Perhaps he washed up somewhere else." He heard the disbelief in his own voice. "He had weak heart. I do not think he would be surviving. If so he will find me, but I am not having any hope." Tentatively Adam spoke. "Your husband was not traveling with you?" "No. He was killed in rioting after mutiny on ship Potemkin. He was an officer. It was massacre. There is much unrest in my Russia." "I'm sorry. Yes, I have read about what is going on there. It sounds difficult." "But it has nothing to do with you, this place so far away from your own country and so you read and think, 'how difficult, how inconvenient. Those peoples should know how to behave. After all if you slap a man down, do not be surprised if he rises up to strike back.'" She had spoken with an intense bitterness that rocked him as if she had struck him in the face. "You freed your serfs and there was a war here in America.
But that was long ago and nothing to do with you. Nothing has anything to do with you." With that she stood slowly gracefully. "Trunk found is mine. I am awake enough to see you lift into boat. Do you think something is dry?"

"It is seeping water. I would not think so. If you would not think it improper, I have some things that might work for you. I'll lay them out by the fire upstairs with some warm water and soap so that you may make such ablutions as you would deem fit." He had spoken formally, stuffily as it were. He had been rebuked and he was indeed "thinking about things." "With your permission." He bowed slightly. He went up the stairs and pulled out his silk nightshirt with his family crest embroidered on it, his brocade dressing gown and some silk socks. He unwrapped the soap his mother had order with the family initial. He laid out his thick Turkish towel and facecloth with the bold D festooned with woven ivy. He drew a pitcher of hot water from the cistern and made everything ready. It was a matter of moments when he returned. "Everything is ready for you. I shall remain down here." He almost said "Your Highness" in mock echo of Sandham, his family's English butler. He watched her as she regally climbed the stair with none of the unbalanced waddle he had observed in other pregnant women. He began to gather up the blanket and pallet to hang to dry in front of the fire. He took the cups to wash. He looked around at the curved room and its sparse furnishings. It was dark. There were no windows cut into the hewn stones. This was the lighthouse keeper's life.

Anouyska stood for a moment by the glowing coal grate upstairs.

She wrapped her arms around herself, hugging herself tightly as if to hold in the emotions that were trying to explode inside of her. All her life her Imperial court training had taught her to show no emotion. Her father had been the same. That gasp on the deck was for him a shriek. When he put his arms around her it was a gesture so unlike him as to be a frantic act to save her. Tears began to flow as she thought of him in those final moments; tears for her father, her mother, her husband, all lost now, all gone. She shook herself and began to remove her sodden clothes. This may have been the first time in her life she had done so without help. There were no servants, no nanny, no lady's maid. Fortunately with the baby there were no stays. That would be too embarrassing for words. She did not even contemplate the thought of that callow young man down the stairs putting a hand on her. She thought such things, but in truth they were of an age, but she had seen more of life than he. That much was obvious. She washed as best she could with the water in the bowl thinking of a steaming bath with hot scented water filled by an army of servants. She wrapped herself in the towel to dry feeling its luxury.

That was a word she did not associate with a lighthouse, not that she had ever thought of lighthouses. For the first time she noticed the towel, the nightshirt of silk, the brocaded robe and matching slippers. Were these things stolen?

Had some rich man's trunk washed up in this place to be found by this lighthouse keeper? The silk was the softest she had ever felt.

The brocade on the robe was rich and deeply woven. Even the slippers were of such workmanship as she had seen only in the Tsar's palace. It was then she noticed the crest on the robe, the initials on the towel, the soap.

As these questions flooded her thoughts the fatigue of her ordeal began to overcome her. She lay on this stranger's bed that at any other time would have been unthinkable and slept.

Adam called softly up to her after a time and then he slowly began to climb the circular stair. He found her there, like the Goldilocks of the story asleep in his bed. He pulled the down comforter from home over her. He stoked the fire. He laid out her clothes to dry, feeling as he did so she would view this as a great liberty. "Women certainly have a lot of clothes." He said softly to himself.

He turned down the lamps and went about his other chores on the list. "What can a lighthouse keeper possibly do all day?" He had said to his father. Now he knew. The list seemed endless.

There was fresh rainwater in a cistern that had to be pumped up, another enormous tank for kerosene for the great lamp and the lanterns that kept the night at bay.

There was coal for the grates to be brought up, a pantry stocked with food, some luxuries added by his mother who didn't want her son to go without the essentials of life, smoked oysters, caviar, stilton cheese, champagne. He smiled as he thought of this. What was there to celebrate on this stark finger of stone on the edge of nowhere? It would be a bleak Christmas. He did at least have some company now. That was something. He pumped, he polished, he swept, he loaded, he scrubbed in this constant battle with salt and damp.

Suddenly he felt a shudder go through the lighthouse. He had never felt that before. He raced to the top where there was a narrow window before coming to the walk at the pinnacle of the tower and looked out. Through the swirling almost blinding snow he could see the waves mounting higher and higher. He turned away as he looked even with the top of one wave, waiting for the impact against the light. It flowed around the stone sweeping around it like a giant army. He went back down the steps. He checked to see that the main door was still secure.

There was water on the bottom floor, but not much. He took the precaution of barring the door with the crossbar that sat in two iron fittings that battened the thick door in place.

He made such things as secure as he could make them and rushed back up to the sitting room.

He stoked the coal here and went softly up the stairs again to do the same in the bedroom where lay his sleeping guest. He turned down the lamps and blew out the tallow candles. Only the golden glow of the coal fire lit the room. It cast its soft refulgence over everything.

He sat in the low rocker by the fire and kept watch over her. For now there was nothing to do, but wait. He dozed, waking to look on the sleeping form and dozing again.

Once he awoke to soft whispers from this mysterious lady. Phrases he could not understand came from her dreams.

Sometimes there were muffled cries that came from painful images racing through her mind. What had she suffered to bring such terror to her sleep? Again he dozed. When next he woke his guest was sitting upright on the bed with the comforter around her. There were dark circles under her eyes, but there was as softness as well. "I am apologizing to you for my incivility toward you. I was thinking you were. . . ." "A peasant? A serf?" Adam replied. "To my shame, yes, this I am thinking." "Why are you doing here?" "Do you mean what am I doing here?" "Da, Yes." "My father wanted me to think about things, that was his phrase and so he paid the old lighthouse keeper to let me keep the light for a while." "But you are wealthy, yes?" "My family is wealthy, yes. We have interests in shipping and coal." "But your father thinks you are not ready for such wealth or such a life as wealth brings?"

He was staggered at her perceptions. "You ask very intrusive questions from one of so short acquaintance." Again the smile hovered on her lips. "Yes, I am in habit of sticking in my nose like the camel. Please forgive. I grew up in Russian Imperial court. There too is a habit of having one's way. I am countess." "And should I call you Countess?"
"I am thinking perhaps since you have carried me here and I am dressed in your nightshirt that you may call me Anouyska." Adam laughed, but it died on his lips when he saw pain on her face. She grabbed her belly and gasped. "Are you all right? Is the baby coming?" "I am well, but the baby is coming sometime soon. I am feeling these contractions for the past week. On ship is not pleasant. It will pass. Not until they are closer do I have to worry. I am trusting God." " Countess. . . Anouyska, forgive me for this impertinence, but are you religious? I saw you bow your head before you ate. Were you praying?" "I am Russian Orthodox, so yes, I am religious, but it is more. I am true believer in Jesus Christ. For me He is more than Icon on the wall surrounded by gold and candles. For me He is real. This you understand?" "I understand, but I am not religious. My father is, my family is, but I am not. I don't see the need."
"You are not seeing the need for God or for belief?" Again he was surprised by her perception. "I look around and see the state of the world. Its evil.

If there is a God why is there evil?" "There is not evil because there is God, there is evil because there is Satan, and man." "Yes, but bad things happen. Good people die, your father, your husband. There are floods, famine, epidemics." "Bad people also die. It is what comes after death that should be in your thoughts. I am remembering something written by Mr. George McDonald in his book <u>At the Back of the North Wind</u>. You know this book?" She asked. "I have heard of Rev. McDonald, but not this book," he replied. In it a young boy speaks to beautiful woman, North Wind. Something bad is happening and boy is sad because North Wind does this. People die. Ship sinks. When boy asks why North Wind who is good causes something bad to happen. North Wind answers, "What do you know of me? Boy answers, "I know only good of you." North Wind says, "That is all there is to know." I believe God is good. He loves me. Even when bad happens I must trust him.
It is like Yusuf in Bible, "You intend for evil, but God meant for good." Always God means for good. For everything there is purpose. This I believe."
"So you think it is good that your husband died, that your father died in this storm that can only be called an act of God?"
"I am not understanding all of the whys of this happening, but it cannot be bad, sad, yes, hard, yes, but not bad."

At that moment another wave crashed against the side of the lighthouse. Adam rushed up to the top of the light to look out of the lone window. Through the snow he could see in the distance the largest wave he had ever seen. It was like a mountain coming out of the distance. He ran back down the stairs and took the Countess by the hand. He dragged her up the stairs to the storage room. "What is happening?" "A wave, a giant wave, another rogue wave like on the ship. We need to get as high as we can in case it floods the lower levels." "But what of people on shore. This wave it will hit them, yes?" "Countess, the only people I care about right now are right here." "NO! The town, you must warn! There must be way." As she spoke the words of the old keeper came to his mind. "If something bad happens, bad weather comes in there's rockets, blue rockets. Fire three of them and get back in the lighthouse if you can." Adam had only an instant to decide. His first thought was himself and then the Countess, but he knew even in his fear and selfishness he could not just do nothing. "Stay here and pray. We'll see what your God will do. Adam ran to the next level where the rockets were stored. There was a box of matches on a shelf. He gathered the rockets and the matches and opened the trap door to the top of the lighthouse. Closing it quickly again behind him. The wind was howling. The snow blinding. What was he thinking? He turned to see how close the wave was now. It was nearly on him.

Even if he managed to get the rockets lit and off there would be no time for him to get back to safety. Fear seized him, but it did not stop him. "I said one lived one's life the best one could and then you died. I just didn't plan on it being so soon." He turned his back to the wave and faced the direction of the shore. He could see nothing. He wedged the rockets in the railings. He crouched and tried the first match. The wind took it. Again he tried, again the match went out. He hunched his shoulders and brought the match as close to him as he could. He struck it and as it flared with it cupped in his hand he lit the three fuses. They sputtered and then took. The sparks cascading down like fireworks. As the rockets ignited he realized he was too close. He squeezed his eyes shut and growled as the rocket flames seared his face. Each rocket shot out into the storm. He unbuckled his belt and buckled it around the iron post. He wrapped his arms around the railings and took a deep breath. The wave was on him. It pulled and ripped at his body. He felt the strain around him as the belt fought against the wave. The salt stung the burns on his face. His lungs were bursting. He wanted to breathe. He wanted to let go, but he held on. His body pummeled by the force of the wave. He wound himself tighter feeling the belt cutting into him and then the wave was gone. He opened his eyes, but he couldn't see. He freed himself from the railings and crawled toward where he thought the trap door should be.

He felt the heat of the great light on his face. It had not gone out. It was still turning, still burning. The surrounding glass had kept out the wave. He felt his way to the door went through and slammed it behind him shooting the bolt. Carefully he made his way down the stairs, feeling his way along with feet and hands. He felt the flatness of the floor. The cold and wet was beginning to set in. His energy gone. He was beginning to shiver in the midst of feeling the burn on his face. The Countess called to him. "Adam, you able to fire rockets? Adam, what has happened?" Adam could not speak for the chattering of his teeth. His shivers were uncontrollable. The rush of adrenaline and the cold were sending him into shock. "Adam!"

The Countess saw in the lamplight the burns on his face, the eyes squeezed shut. She embraced him as hard as she could, giving him the warmth of her body. It was difficult with the baby. Slowly the shivering left him, but he still had difficulty speaking. She led him down the spiral stairs and wrapped him in a blanket. She stoked the fire and put more coal on the hearth. She guided him to the fire and stood him in front of it. "You cannot see?" "Rockets" was his only answer. She knew then what had happened. She pressed some of the left over broth to his lips and some brandy as well. She took the blanket away and began to remove his shirt, his shoes. When he resisted she became "You will die if you are not kept warm and dry.

Now is my turn to save you, yes?" He yielded to her ministrations and soon found himself in dry clothes beside the fire, but still he could not see. Anouyska found some blue salve and spread it over the burns on his face. She bandaged his eyes, taking the cloth slowly, but tightly around his head. His speech returned and he told her what had happened. He had fired the rockets. The blast had blinded him. Bitterness crept into his voice. "No good deed should go unpunished." "What you are saying. You save lives. It is good thing you do." "Only if it worked. Otherwise I'm blind for nothing." "Doing good thing is not nothing. It is good thing. My husband die in mutiny defending nation. It was not for nothing. Good will come." The storm had continued to batter the lighthouse. Wave after wave crashed against the granite structure but not as high as the wave that swept over Adam. "I need to keep the light. There are chores to do. I. . . I cannot see. Would you. . . can you guide me?" "I will do this." Anouyska led him over the lighthouse from top to bottom still wrapped in his dressing gown and slippers. She put his hands on the pumps. She guided his steps. She was careful, tender.

He asked her to look out of the lone window. "Still is snowing. Now is night. I see many flakes when light passes. It is like Moscow. It is your Christmas Eve. We celebrate." "Countess Anouyska, I'm blind. My face is burned. We are trapped on an island in a blizzard. What is there to celebrate?" "You live, I live. You save town.

Is Christmas! Is good!" Now it was his turn to smile. He felt the tightness in his skin with the burns. His hand went slowly to his eyes his fingers roamed gingerly over the bandages. There was discomfort, but no real pain. "What do you mean, 'it is my Christmas Eve?" "Russian Orthodox celebrate old Christmas January 7 according to old calendar. So is good is your Christmas otherwise would fast. Now we eat. What is to eat?" Anouyska asked. We could celebrate if you like. "With soup in broken cups?" She said. Champagne and caviar for Christmas." He answered. "You have caviar?" "Beluga, from Russia. My mother's idea. Champagne, caviar, smoked oysters, smoked salmon. All the comforts of home without the tree. We have no Christmas tree, unless one washes up on the railings by the light, which could happen tonight." "I will make tree." And with that she took her father's umbrella opened the bare frame and put it in the stand for the fire tools. She then went to her trunk opened it and began to remove its sodden contents. "I will hang to dry later. This we will put on tree."

She drew out from the trunk her jewelry case and opened it in all its sparkling beauty.

She began to hang the diamonds, emeralds and rubies on the umbrella frame. He could not see this, but she described each one as she hung it so that in his mind he saw the brilliant panoply of jewels and color caught in the firelight. "I have something for the tree as well. "Adam said.

He shuffled over to the crate where he had stored his trove of shells from his daily outing. With his hands he found the starfish, stiff and dry by now, but beautifully white in his hand. "Here, for the top." Anouyska took the delicate body carefully in her hands and placed it leaning against the point on the frame. Both of them were working very hard at keeping up a brave face for the other. "Tell me of your Christmas, Adam." "We have a tree. It is lit by candles, so we only light it on Christmas Eve for a little while and again on Christmas morning. We decorate it ourselves."
"This I do not understand." She questioned. "I mean we put on the decorations. We have some friends who have their servants do everything. They just sort of sit back and occasionally give directions. My mother says that is the height of laziness." "Yes, I am thinking so too, even though some things I have servants do you perhaps think is lazy too." "Like what?" "You are never minding. Go on." "Well, we usually have a party in the afternoon for all the servants and their families with lots of food and presents. It is great fun. Mother has caterers in for that. She says what good is it to have a party for the servants if all they are doing is making work for themselves. We may do a little visiting after that. Then friends come by to visit us. There are presents. Mother keeps food on the sideboard in the dining room so we graze ourselves through the evening." "What is grazing?" "Eating, but more like cows." "Ah, grazing, yes. In Russia too there is grazing."

"Then everybody sits by the fireplace where our stockings are hung for St. Nicklaus and Father reads the Christmas story from the book of Luke." "This we also do. I can read now if you like. There is Bible beside bed." "Can you read English?" "Yes, I am reading English. My nurse was French so I am speaking French. My riding instructor was Spanish, so I am speaking Spanish. My fencing master is German, so I am speaking German. My governess is English, so I am speaking English and reading English. What do you speak?" "I speak Yale which is thought by some to be a form of English." "I am not understanding." "Never mind. Yes, please read the Christmas story. After that we open one present and by then it's pretty late so we go to bed until St. Nicklaus comes on Christmas morning."

"I am reading now Christmas story in Luke chapter 2."

Luke 2 ¹And it came to pass in those days, that there went out a decree from Caesar Augustus that all the world should be taxed. ²(And this taxing was first made when Cyrenius was governor of Syria.) ³And all went to be taxed, every one into his own city. ⁴And Joseph also went up from Galilee, out of the city of Nazareth, into Judaea, unto the city of David, which is called Bethlehem; (because he was of the house and lineage of David:) ⁵To be taxed with Mary his espoused wife, being great with child. ⁶And so it was, that, while they were there, the days were accomplished that she should be delivered. ⁷And she brought forth her firstborn son, and wrapped him in swaddling clothes, and laid him in a manger; because

there was no room for them in the inn. [8]And there were in the same country shepherds abiding in the field, keeping watch over their flock by night.
[9]And, lo, the angel of the Lord came upon them, and the glory of the Lord shone round about them: and they were sore afraid. [10]And the angel said unto them, Fear not: for, behold, I bring you good tidings of great joy, which shall be to all people. [11]For unto you is born this day in the city of David a Savior, which is Christ the Lord. [12]And this shall be a sign unto you; Ye shall find the babe wrapped in swaddling clothes, lying in a manger. [13]And suddenly there was with the angel a multitude of the heavenly host praising God, and saying, [14]Glory to God in the highest, and on earth peace, good will toward men. [15]And it came to pass, as the angels were gone away from them into heaven, the shepherds said one to another, Let us now go even unto Bethlehem, and see this thing which is come to pass, which the Lord hath made known unto us. [16]And they came with haste, and found Mary, and Joseph, and the babe lying in a manger. [17]And when they had seen it, they made known abroad the saying which was told them concerning this child. [18]And all they that heard it wondered at those things which were told them by the shepherds. [19]But Mary kept all these things, and pondered them in her heart. [20]And the shepherds returned, glorifying and praising God for all the things that they had heard and seen, as it was told unto them."

Anouyska slowly closed the Bible. "Is beautiful story, yes?" "I have always liked the Bible stories. I grew up on them. David and Goliath. Daniel and the Lion's den. The story of the little boy with the loaves and fishes. The healing of the blind man. I know now how he must have felt." They were silent for a moment as this sank in.

"Mother read all those stories to us when we were children. I've always thought the Bible had a beauty of language about it. I like the way it sounds." "Yes, I am hearing these stories from a little girl also. My favorite was Hebrew children in fiery furnace. Perhaps because it is so cold in Russia. I thought how nice to be so warm." They both laughed at her small joke. "Anouyska, what do you do for Christmas?" "Well, first we are fasting. We do not eat, but then we do. On Christmas Eve there is no meat. We eat porridge called kutya, from wheat berries with honey and poppy seeds. All this means for us hope and eternity with happiness, and rest. There is blessing of home and everyone eat from same dish for family. Some people take spoon of kutya and throw on ceiling. If stick is good harvest, but we are not doing such thing. Very messy. We have a "Holy Supper with 12 foods for twelve apostles. Mushroom soup, bread, honey, garlic, codfish, fruit like apricots, figs or dates, nuts, beans with potatoes, peas, potatoes with parsley, bobal'ki, (is small biscuit with poppy seed and honey, and red wine. Then there are the kolyadki. They dress like the animals in Bible, cows, sheep, goat, camel and sing songs about Christ child. Is much fun. I wanted to be a lamb kolyadki when I was girl. We give them food or money and they go to next house. Sometimes we would have more than one group of kolyadki come to house. Father would give money to all, even if they were not good singers.

'Is Christmas' he would say." "So if the food represents the twelve Apostles, which one is Judas?" "I am thinking it must be garlic, because never know when it will betray you."

Again they laughed, but this time it was more real for them. Slowly they were becoming friends, not just strangers thrown together by the storm. "We eat now, yes, because the baby is getting very hungry." Adam told her where to find everything and soon the small table was laid out with all the luxuries Adam's mother had packed for him. As they ate they talked more and more freely about their lives. The Edwardian reserves that surrounded both of them slowly dropped away. Adam's blindness made him keenly aware of the tastes, sounds and smells around him. He could smell the light scent Anouyska had sprayed on when she opened her trunk. Anouyska could study Adam now that he could not see her gaze. Already she saw more of the man and less of the boy in him. His ordeal had matured him, his blindness softened him. The time passed and soon the light demanded attention.

Again Anouyska led Adam through the routine that had become so familiar to him over the past weeks. When the chores were complete they again sat and Anouyska asked, "Shall I make tea?" "Yes, please. Tea would feel good on a cold night. Anouyska heated the pot with hot water. She brewed the tea and poured it into the chipped cups.

With sugar and tinned milk it was comforting and sweet. They sat in comfortable silence, enjoying the tea. Adam heard the tea cup shatter on the floor. He heard Anouyska's gasp and sharp intake of breath. "Baby is coming!" "Now?" Adam exclaimed. "Soon! Soon!" Adam could hear the strain in her voice. He stood not knowing what to do. "I am going up to the bedroom. You are following me now." Anouyska said imperiously and they went. She grabbed his hand. She was squeezing him so tightly his fingers hurt. He stumbled after her up the stairway. Another groan left her. She squeezed tighter still on his hand. Then another groan. "Water is broken. We hurry!" She made her way to the bed and collapse on it. He could hear the rustle of fabric. Another groan, this time almost a growl. "What is happening? What can I do?" Adam said. "What is happening is baby! What you are doing is catching baby!" "I can't. I mean. I'm not, we're not. . ." "Catch baby!" Anouyska screamed. Adam knelt by the bed.

He could hear Anouyska's breathing, the primal groans that came as she strained. He reached out and felt her ankles. "Now wait!" She growled. "I am pushing. Baby is coming." Again he heard a deep intake of air and again he heard her strain. Again and again she did this. He could hear her speaking softly through the strain. It sounded like prayer, but it was in Russian. He could feel the sweat from her ankles. Her muscles were trembling. The strain continued.

He heard a deep growl come from Anouyska then she screamed, "Catch baby!" Slowly tentatively he put out his hands and felt the warm wetness of the newborn. He could feel its struggles in his hands. He found his handkerchief and wiped the face. When he lifted it up he could feel the tug of the umbilicus. He sensed Anouyska raising up, leaning forward. He felt small movements through the cord. He heard the sound of scissors and then Anouyska's tired voice whisper, "Give baby to me.

He felt her hands around his own as she took her child. He sat back. He had never experienced anything so real. He realized he was sobbing although his eyes were bound by the bandages. He heard the soft cry of the baby, the gentle murmur of Anouyska to comfort. "Is boy." She said softly. "Is baby boy. I shall call him Pietro Alexandraovich Kilkhoff, for his father and for the Czar. Is good name." "He is a Christmas baby, Anouyska. It is Christmas Eve, just on midnight." Adam said through his sobs. "Adam, are you crying? Why are you crying?" "That was the most real thing I have ever experienced. We are not husband and wife.

He is not my baby, but I wonder if that is what Joseph felt all those Christmases ago. It was pure joy. It was overwhelming." "Yes, it is whelming over. I am sleeping now, so is baby." Adam could hear the fatigue in her voice and soon he heard her soft breathing along with the small grunts and soft noises of a new born.

He felt for the edges of the blanket and pulled them up around Anouyska and the baby, feeling her outline with his hands. Adam felt his way back over to the chair and again feeling the heat of the fire tossed a few pieces of coal on to the glowing grate. He sank back into the chair and nodded off. He was skiing in Vermont. He could feel the wind on his cheeks and the cold biting his eyes. Suddenly everything went black and he could not see. He began to tumble, the sensation of falling sweeping over him. "Adam. Adam. Adam, you are dreaming. You must be waking now. Is time for the light."

Anouyska soft whisper brought him gently to the surface. He remembered where he was and what had happened. "Pietro is sleeping now. I have fed him. He is good. We will care for light, yes?" Again he went through the weary routine that had almost become second nature to him. Anouyska guided his hands to the pumps, his feet to the steps. Up and down, back and forth. Again he slept. It seemed a place out of time. "Is still snowing. Morning comes soon." Each of them dozed, he in the chair, her in the bed with the baby. This time he woke first.

He felt his way through the room to his steamer trunks. Quietly he opened the lid. He began to search with his hands the items he knew were there. First one thing and then another. He found the Christmas stocking he knew his mother had packed there and the few small presents she had secreted away for Christmas Day.

He slowly made his way down to the kitchen where he put water on for coffee. He set bread to toast on the hob. He didn't think he was up to making eggs without his sight just yet, "I might have to learn." He peeled the oranges his mother had sent. He got out the butter. He opened the box of almonds. He got out the honey. When everything was ready he put it on a tray made from an old crate top he found and slowly crept up the steps to the bedroom above. He could hear the baby nursing. "Someone is hungry this morning." "So is someone else. What do you have? Coffee? Toast? Oranges, lovely." He felt her hands on his. "Here, I will take tray." Anouyska sat looking at him with his sightless eyes. His face smiling, expectant. "Of what are you thinking, Adam?" "It's Christmas Day. And whatever I might have expected when my father arranged this adventure sitting here with you was never a part of it." "For me also," she replied. "Never when we set sail for America was I thinking of this, but for you there is something else I think, yes?" "Anouyska, on Christmas morning we open presents. I wanted to give you something, something for you and for the baby." He reached behind his chair and brought out several packaged roughly wrapped in old newspaper. It was all he had. He had tied them with string, the uneven tails a testimony to his lack of sight. He gently reached out toward her and felt her hands as she cupped his. "Thank you, I am thanking you so very much.

What wonderful surprise! May I open them now?" "Yes, yes!" Eagerly she began to tear away the wrapping on the first present. He could hear her purr with anticipation as she freed the gift. He could not see which one she had chosen first. He was as eager as she to see what she had chosen. "Adam! Adam, what is this?" "You'll have to tell me what it looks like first." "Is pin with big rock on top held with prongs." "That is a stick pin. It is for holding a man's tie, but I thought you could use it to hold your scarf in place." "But what is rock?" "It's a gold nugget from our family mines in California. I had it made for myself, so it is mine to give. I think on me it would be too much, but for a Countess from Russia it should be just right. Open the others." One by one she opened the presents.

When she was finished tears streamed from her eyes. Laid out before her was another stick pin with a diamond in its golden prongs, a star ruby ring. There were two collar pins that would serve as diaper pins for the baby and a gold watch fob chain that wrapped twice around her wrist.

"Adam, I cannot take these things from you." "Please, you must." He said. "I have nothing else and it would give me great pleasure for you to accept them." "But it is not proper. These gifts are too great for me. Yes, there is much between us in short time, but these are too much." "Please, take them. Take them for a time when it will not be improper for you to take them." "I am not understanding you." "Take them."

"But for you also there must be gifts." Anouyska went to her trunk, now slowly drying and somewhat emptied of its contents now draped about the lighthouse. He felt something soft surround his neck. His hands felt its luxurious softness. "Is scarf of cashmere. Is dark blue. It will keep you warm when you tend the light. And Adam this also is for you." She pressed a watch into his hand. "This was belonging to my grandfather. Is Breugette. Listen." He felt her open the lid and the sweetest chime filled his ears. "Is the hour. This will chime the hour and half hour so even if you cannot see, you will know time." "I cannot take this. This is for your son, your family." "No, Adam, is for you. This also is for you." She pressed a braided cord into his hands. "Is fob for watch. Is woven from my hair." "Then it is purest gold indeed, Anouyska."

She blushed at his tone and was thankful he could not see. "Here is one thing more." She reached for his hand and wrapped his fingers around something smooth and heavy. "This is cane also from my grandfather. Head is gold, shaft is ebony. It will help you as you walk, yes?" "Yes." Adam said quietly.

They sat like shy children quietly for a time each not knowing exactly what to say, what to do.

"Anouyska, I am falling in love with you." "I am loving you also, Adam." "Is this too soon? Is this proper?" "I am not knowing what is soon and what is proper, Adam. I am only knowing that I have not felt such feelings before.

My husband was a good man and very kind, but in Russia, marriages for Countesses are not for love. It was thought a good match and so it was, but what I am feeling for you, this is love." These thoughts rested between them like a glowing ember. Warm, comforting, quiet. Anouyska fed baby Peter, changing him with one of the towels cut small. She laid him down and went about the task of keeping the light. Growing in Adam's heart and head was the knowledge that with his love for Anouyska came the understanding of Jesus Christ, His birth, His death and His resurrection. When they finished the chores and Anouyska had guided him gently back to the chair by the grate he took both her hands in his. "Anouyska, how do I come to God? How do I, it sounds so strange, become a Christian? How do I 'get saved' as the Bible thumpers say?" Tears welled up in Anouyska's eyes as she heard the belief in his voice.
"You must tell God you are sinner." "I know that well enough!" "And you are asking Jesus Christ to be Savior to you. Then you are becoming a child of God." "Yes, I've heard my mother say those words and our pastor. I guess I know what to say and do growing up attending church with my parents. I just needed to say it." "So now you are doing this?" "Yes, Anouyska, now I am doing this."

And with that he bowed his head and his heart and with moving lips that made no sound he accepted the gift of Christmas, the Christ-child, crucified, buried and risen to pay the debt for his sin. He held Anouyska close. She could feel the sobs against his chest as he felt the forgiveness of God fill his heart. She too was crying tears of joy. They held each other close for a very long time. She pulled slowly away. "Now is time for Peter again. You are waiting here. I will get him and read for you from Bible, yes?" "Yes, and then it will be time to tend the light." They sat together by the fire, Adam listening for the first time to the beauty of the truth instead of the beauty of the words. The Bible was to him now more than good literature. They had finished the chores again in the now familiar pattern of Anouyska leading, placing Adam's hands to pump and turn and haul and pull. Each task in its ordered time. His heart rejoiced each time he felt her hands upon his, each time he felt her closeness. Her warmth spread through him like a healing balm.

Day passed into night as the routine rolled on: feeding, changing the baby, sleeping, tending the light, doing the chores. The storm passed in the night as all storms do and the next day broke cold and clear with a rime of ice from the sea coating the light.

They were at the railing cleaning the glass when Anouyska spoke, "Adam, there is boat coming." "Sail or steam?" "There is smoke and how do you say, chimney?" "Stack?"

"Yes, stack, there is smoking stack." Adam smiled at her words. "How far away?" "There are peoples, but I am not seeing their faces." "We'll go down and welcome them."
They set off down the circular stairs of the lighthouse, Adam slowly feeling his way along the now familiar way. Anouyska gathered up baby Peter and wrapped him against the cold of the lower level where there was no fire. Adam felt his way to the door and lifted the heavy bar resting in the iron angles. He swung open the door and felt the sun upon his face. He could hear the steam engine now, its sound carrying across the water. A horn sounded announcing their arrival. The boat was closer now. He heard the murmur of voices as the boat drew nearer. He heard the command to let go the anchor and the soft splash as a boat lowered into the water. "Adam? Adam?" It was his father's deep voice. "Papa, I hear you," he called. The boat scraped against the rocks and he heard a footfall as his father leaped from the boat ahead of the sailors rowing it. "Adam, are you all right?
What's wrong with your eyes? What has happened?" "Papa, this is the Countess Anouyska Kilkhoff and her son, Peter. Countess, this is my father, Mr. Adam Blakely Dennett Sr."
Habit of manners took over for a moment as the introductions were made and acknowledged. "What has happened? The city saw the flairs and got people away from the shore.

Ships were washed up blocks inland, houses destroyed, but no lives lost when the wave hit. Your mother, sisters and I were safe on the hill. We couldn't get out here until today. I brought the launch and the old keeper. He was worried about what you had done to his light."

At that moment the keeper pushed past all of them and began to inspect his precious lighthouse. They could hear him muttering to himself as he climbed the stairs. "Papa, the Countess washed up just before Christmas Eve. Her ship had been sunk by a rogue wave." His father nodded. Bodies had begun to wash up. "I found her and brought her here. The storm was coming and I saw the wave. I lit the blue rockets just in time, but I was too close and the blast from the rockets blinded me. The Countess bandaged my eyes and helped me keep the light. The baby was born right after that." His father looked at both of them in some amazement as the import of all this broke over him. He ushered them in out of the cold and shepherded them up the circular stairs into the sitting room. Anouyska placed the baby in the box they had been using as a cradle and began to make tea in a practiced manner. Adam's father stared at his son in silence.

The old lighthouse keeper broke in on their reverie. "By gum, young feller, you kept her. You kept her alright! I thought she'd be a wreck and I didn't know what to think when I saw them blue lights except that it warn't good.

I run like a rabbit when I seen everyone else runnin'. But by gum, you done good keeping the light."
"Are you ready to go home, Son? Your mother has been so worried. We need to get you to a specialist. We'll see what can be done."
"Whatever it is, Papa it will be alright. It is God's will. I know that now, but Papa, where ever I am going, Anouyska will be joining me." "Is that your wish, Countess?" "Yes, Mr. Dennett, that is my wish also. I will tell you my story along the way if you wish it."
"I think I'd like that very much. I see that much has happened to my son since he has been away." "Thinking about things, Papa? Thinking about things." "Yes." Everything was packed away. They were on the launch motoring their way against the ebbing tide back to the shore. Adam turned to Anouyska his arm circling her waist as she held the baby. "Adam, the light it is still shining." "Yes, beloved, the light is still shining."

THE END

5 OUTBACK CHRISTMAS 1930

"Christmas should not be this blasted hot." The words echoed through her head like a chant. The sun beat down on her like a bludgeon. Every step stirred the red dust of the Outback into a cloud that settled over her hat, her clothes, her swollen body like a blanket. It stuck to the sweat in red rivulets like blood streaming down her flesh. She could feel the grit in her teeth and taste the dirt on her tongue. How did her life ever come to this? Pregnant, alone, walking on a deserted road miles from anywhere in a country half the world away from home. She and Steven had left home to start over after the market crash in '29 to find a better life after they had lost everything. Starting over, starting over in their marriage, their lives. But their life hadn't started over. Her father's words came back to her, "If you're not happy with who you are, you will never be happy with where you are no matter what you do."

Steven bought an opal mine through an agent, sold her jewels and mortgaged what little they owned to get them to this god-forsaken place with dreams of opals laying on the ground like manna from heaven and a euphoria that burst like a bubble when they saw the empty hole in the ground they had purchased. It had been a swindle from start to finish. Now she was pregnant and alone. Steven was dead, killed in a cave-in because they couldn't even afford the boards to shore up what little mine they had dug. They had dug it. She whose hands had once been called lovely, hands that were made for wearing diamonds and gracing the keys of the grand piano the bailiffs had carted off with everything else. Now her hands were as rough and calloused as her soul. Still she walked on, heat shimmering off the track and the red earth around her.

As she walked her mind played back the images over the last months like the black and white "news of the day" that came on before the main feature at the Palace Cinema in Sydney. Steven had lavishly booked first class passage to Australia. They sailed into Sydney Harbor like millionaires. Then came the disappointment when the investment turned literally to dust. Steven got another claim, but it too was empty of opals. The government paid a shilling a foot just for digging so they had lived on that, digging just to eat. Then the pregnancy, the doctor smiling as he delivered the news, frowning when she asked if she could get rid of "it".

"No, young lady, I cannot get rid of IT. I suggest you look forward to this coming child."
She and Steven had gotten an invitation from one of her father's business acquaintances in Melbourne for the Melbourne Cup. They scraped together the train fare and stayed with the man in his mansion, living like princes in the last of their finery left from the old days, looking out over Phillip Bay from St. Kilda. Even though she was eight months pregnant she was determined to go the Cup and enjoy herself. She made one of her old frocks work around her belly, put a hat on her head and paraded out as if she were at Royal Ascot on derby day. She had gotten looks from some, but she didn't care. For a time the ruin was forgotten and she was a young heiress from Connecticut again like the days when Steven had courted her. A smile curled around her lips as the memory floated through her parched brain. Phar Lap had won the Cup. They had danced and celebrated as if they themselves were the owners. "Maybe one day!" Steven had shouted over the crowd. Then Steven had gambled away their winnings and if she hadn't purchased return tickets they would have been stranded without anything. Her father's business acquaintance's generosity lasted until Steven asked him for money. Not even the rich had money to lend after the crash.
Her steps were slower now and the heat was bearing down even more. She had forgotten water, but then she hadn't planned to need any.

She was going to walk into the wilderness until she passed out and then she would die, the child inside of her dying with her. She trudged on, the smile fading quickly. She could see her father. He was walking toward her. Beside him was their butler, Childers, carrying a tray with a tall pitcher of lemonade, the water beading on its cold opulence. There was food on the tray, tea cakes and watercress sandwiches. Her father was dressed in his suit of white linen, Childers in his uniform. Just like the old days. She could see the ice in the glass beside the pitcher. She was a girl again and it was summer in Newport. Her brow came together as she struggled with the image. It was hot, but not July. She wasn't home, she was in Australia. She had something she must do, but she couldn't remember what it was. Closer now, she could almost touch the pitcher. She could hear the ice tinkling in the cut glass pitcher and then blackness.

"Is she dead?" Elizabeth heard the precise vowels of England as she wondered where she was. She was in a cool dark place laying on something soft. Gentle hands were cooling her face with a wet cloth. There was a humming, cooing sound coming from an aborigine woman. "No sir, baby coming soon though. Maybe tonight, maybe tomorrow. She in a bad way now." Sweet oblivion swept over her as dreams and memory merged into Elizabeth's mind. Images of her father, her mother, her family rolled through her thoughts. She drifted. She slept.

Slowly awareness came back to her. She was in Australia. She was pregnant. She was alone. She wanted to die. "You passed out on the track just south of the ridge. Peggy found you and brought you here. Is there someone we can send for? Husband? Family? Friends?" These words were spoken in caring tones. More care than she had heard in a long time.
Her lips were cracked, her throat dry. It was hard to speak. She managed a raspy whisper."No one." "What were you doing out there, by yourself, no food, no water in this heat? You could have died" said Neville. "That was my plan." rasped Elizabeth. "Ah, didn't do such a good job then did you? The soft sarcasm of England coming through. "Do you have a name?" "I'm Elizabeth, Elizabeth Windom Garrett." "Right, I'm Neville, this young lady is Peggy." "You're welcome here until you, until. . . well, you're welcome here. Right then. I've got to get back to work. Mines don't dig themselves." Neville strode out. Elizabeth rolled slowly to her side, her pregnant belly rolling with her. Her child heavy inside, restless in its confinement. She could see her skin rise and fall, little movements. Every now and again a kick would jolt her. There was a human being inside her. "He getting ready to come out soon. You'll see." Peggy smiled, her white teeth flashing in the dark room. "Goin' to be a fine little joey. You are called Miss Elizabeth.

My name is Penkara, that means 'hawk' in my language, but Mr. Neville calls me Peggy because he think Penkara sound funny. "Peggy,. . . Peggy, where am I?" Elizabeth sighed. "You'm be in Lightening Ridge. In Mr. Neville Blackstone's house under the ground at his opal mine and a good thing too. Mr. Neville's a good man. Lotta yabbos chasing around out there, robbers and ratters. You come to a good place to have your baby." Silent tears began to stream down Elizabeth's face. She was having a baby. She was having a baby. She had planned to die in the dust and now she was having a baby. It was Christmas Eve. The day passed. Peggy told Elizabeth about finding her along the track.

How she dragged Elizabeth to Mr. Neville's house because that's where Peggy worked. Peggy had washed the dust from Elizabeth's body and dressed her in one of Mr. Neville's night shirts.

Mr. Neville don't use no night shirt no more he just fall into bed clothes and all. I love Mr. Neville like he was my family. Mr. Neville rescued me. I was drunken all the time. He found me in Sydney begging for whisky and selling myself. He just helped me up and took me to a church where some nice people took care of me and he left money to feed me and help me. A good Samaritan he was. When I had sobered up and was Peggy again he said he needed a house keeper only he didn't have a house exactly and did I want a job. And here I am and I don't get drunk no more."

All this streamed out of Peggy in a pleasant, humorous flow as Peggy cared for Elizabeth as if she were a little child. Elizabeth could see Peggy's broad nose, dark skin topped by a thatch of hair bleached orange by the Sun, and her kind eyes as she slowly moved about bringing food, getting water. "Peggy, what do I do with this baby when I have it? She asked. "Love that baby! You got to love that baby. I had a baby once and the government come and took him away. That's why I was drinking. I don't know where my boy is now. You love that baby, everything else you figure out along the way." Elizabeth truly had no idea what to do with a baby. She was reared by nannies and governesses. When her own baby brother was born she was just a child and he died so soon after he came into the world she had little memory of him. When her second brother came along she was too grown up to care about him. It was too much to take in. She slept again to the soft crooning of Peggy moving peacefully about and then all was quiet.

Elizabeth flew up with a cry on her lips and such a pain as she had never felt. The baby was coming. Neville rushed in the room took one look and ran out shouting for Peggy. Peggy came back in and took Elizabeth by the hand. "It's going to be all right now . . . all right now. The baby's coming, and just in time for Christmas too. "Peggy whispered. "Just like the baby Jesus in the crèche, in the manger."

"I'll get the district nurse" shouted Neville. "No time for the nurse, this baby's coming right now." Peggy retorted. "What do we do?" "Boil some water to keep things clean and pray. Her body will do the rest," said Peggy. A low groaning growl escaped from Elizabeth and Neville fled from the room. The baby came as babies do and after the turmoil Elizabeth marveled at this tiny being nursing at her breast. Peggy had washed the baby and bathed Elizabeth, found cloth for a diaper and a fresh night shirt for her. "What you going to call him?" Peggy asked. A name. . . Elizabeth had not thought about a name. All she had thought about was ending her life, his life as well, not about a name for this helpless bundle now sleeping nestled on her chest. In the quiet she heard the sound of a victrola playing Christmas music. "Sleep in Heavenly Peace". . . . then "Good King Wenceslas", how about Wenceslas? No! At that moment a choir began to scratchily sing "the first Noel the angels did sing". What about Noel? "His name is Noel." Peggy nodded, "For Christmas! For the Christ child born on Christmas Day." Elizabeth smiled weakly. Peggy went on about how Jesus was born in a cave and all the shepherd came. Elizabeth knew the Christmas story because her family had always gone to church when she was a child, but it had been a long time since she had thought about Jesus or heard those words, "Christ Child," a long time since she had given any thought to the God she had learned about as a child.

Just then Neville entered with a tray and two of the most beautiful cut crystal goblets she had ever seen.
"I thought a toast might be in order. Wet the baby's head and all that. "She's going to call him Noel," Peggy said "To Noel!" "To Noel" She said softly.
As she tasted the wine, its red darkness smooth on her tongue she thought how odd that in the midst of Australia at a place called Lightening Ridge in a hole in the ground wearing a borrowed night shirt she should be toasting her new born child with wine served in cut crystal goblets poured from a crystal decanter. "Where did all this come from?" She asked. "I've been saving it for when I strike it rich. This seemed like as good an occasion as any, but the rest of it is a long story for another time. Right now you and Noel need your rest. It's almost time for Father Christmas. Happy Christmas! Good night. Sleep well. Give a shout if you need anything."
Neville left. Peggy curled up in a chair in the corner of the room and was soon softly snoring. Elizabeth eased the baby to her side and slept.
She awoke slowly to a smell of coffee and wrapped herself in the languor of the moment. She remembered waking in the night to nurse the baby and again when Peggy took him to change his nappy as the Aussies called diapers, but she had not felt such peace as she had now in this place for a long time. Noel was sleeping. She slowly eased herself up and began to look around.

Yesterday was another time and place. Everything was a blur in her mind. Her eyes roved over the smooth red walls of the room scattered with English hunting prints. The furniture was quite fine, even the bed in which she lay was ornately carved from mahogany. Everything around her was completely at odds with its setting. This was an underground room, dug out of the red outback earth, but what was in it was quite fine. Peggy came in with a silver tray laden with food; fruit, porridge, juice and real coffee. "Good morning, Miss Elizabeth, how are you feeling? How is the baby? You haven't even seen what Father Christmas left you last night." As she spoke Peggy put down the tray and lifted two old red socks hanging at the foot of the bed.

"See what Father Christmas brought you and the baby too." Peggy laid the socks gently in Elizabeth's lap. Elizabeth felt the wonder swelling inside her like the Christmas morning excitement of her childhood. With her lower lip between her teeth and the light of anticipation in her eyes she slowly put her hand into the first sock and brought out a small silver spoon emblazoned with a crest. Then a tiny cup and a sterling baby rattle wrapped in a flannel pouch. She gasped softly when she saw the silver and tears began to fill her eyes. She turned to her own stocking and there drew out an orange, a handkerchief embroidered with small purple flowers and scented with lavender.

There were two small lavender sachets and at the very bottom carefully wrapped were the two crystal glasses from the night before. Tears were now streaming down her face. She had not known such kindness since she left home years before. How could such things be? "Oh, Peggy, I have nothing for you or Mr. Neville." "You have the baby; he is a gift to all of us. Your coming to us is a gift. Besides, we don't need much. When you've finished breakfast and feel up to it, Mr. Neville says please join us in the Drawing Room as he calls it." Elizabeth marveled again as she ate and made herself presentable in what could only be a dressing gown again appropriated from Mr. Neville. She scooped up Noel and slowly made her way through the house following the sound of Christmas music from the victrola. "Happy Christmas!" smiled Neville. "Come and sit, I would say, by the fire, but we don't have one and certainly don't need one today." The Drawing Room had lovely furniture, oil lamps and one of the most anemic trees she had ever seen.

"Sorry about the tree and all that, but your New England blue spruce don't do well down under and a eucalyptus was the best I could find on short notice."

"It has a wonderful smell, but what are the decorations?"

"Opals, black opals. It's all I had to put on the tree."

The tree was covered in small rough pieces of black opal hung on wires that danced and shimmered in the lamplight. "They're not worth much as opals go, but I had them lying around." Elizabeth went to the tree and cupped one of the opals in her hand. This is what all the fuss was about. This stone was why she had left home to seek a fortune and here they were hanging on the scraggliest tree she had ever seen. She smiled at the thought. "Please, sit." Neville added. "We have a tradition on Christmas mornings to read the Christmas story from the Bible before we open presents. I hope you'll join us, please." Elizabeth sat cradling Noel in her arms. Peggy sat with her on the settee tucking her bare feet under her. Neville smiled, cleared his throat and began to read. LUKE 2

1 ¶ And it came to pass in those days, that there went out a decree from Caesar Augustus, that all the world should be taxed.

2 (And this taxing was first made when Cyrenius was governor of Syria.)3 And all went to be taxed, every one into his own city.

4 And Joseph also went up from Galilee, out of the city of Nazareth, into Judaea, unto the city of David, which is called Bethlehem; (because he was of the house and lineage of David:)

5 To be taxed with Mary his espoused wife, being great with child.6 And so it was, that, while they were there, the days were accomplished that she should be delivered.

7 And she brought forth her firstborn son, and wrapped him in swaddling clothes, and laid him in a manger; because there was no room for them in the inn.

8 ¶ And there were in the same country shepherds

Christmas Time

abiding in the field, keeping watch over their flock by night. 9 And, lo, the angel of the Lord came upon them, and the glory of the Lord shone round about them: and they were sore afraid. 10 And the angel said unto them, Fear not: for, behold, I bring you good tidings of great joy, which shall be to all people. 11 For unto you is born this day in the city of David a Saviour, which is Christ the Lord. 12 And this shall be a sign unto you; Ye shall find the babe wrapped in swaddling clothes, lying in a manger. 13 And suddenly there was with the angel a multitude of the heavenly host praising God, and saying, 14 Glory to God in the highest, and on earth peace, good will toward men. 15 And it came to pass, as the angels were gone away from them into heaven, the shepherds said one to another, Let us now go even unto Bethlehem, and see this thing which is come to pass, which the Lord hath made known unto us. 16 And they came with haste, and found Mary, and Joseph, and the babe lying in a manger. 17 And when they had seen it, they made known abroad the saying which was told them concerning this child. 18 And all they that heard it wondered at those things which were told them by the shepherds.
19 But Mary kept all these things, and pondered them in her heart. 20 And the shepherds returned, glorifying and praising God for all the things that they had heard and seen, as it was told unto them.

Neville closed the Bible and prayed a prayer beautiful in its sweetness and simplicity for Peggy and for Elizabeth and Noel. It had been a long time since anyone had prayed for Elizabeth. Not since her father had held her in his arms just before he gave her away at the wedding. She had been embarrassed and had laughed at him. She wasn't laughing now. She was in wonder.

"Now, presents! Peggy is positively standing on her head to open presents" said Neville. "Mr. Neville, everyone in Australia is standing on their heads, are we not on the bottom of the world, turned upside down? But opening presents is very nice." "I'll be Father Christmas, shall I?" As Neville spoke he took a tiny wrapped package from under the tree and gave it to Peggy. She opened it. It was a gold cross. "I found the gold fossiking last winter down an old abandoned gold mine in Ballarat and had it made for you." There was a delicate gold chain to go with it. "Oh, Mr. Neville, it is lovely. Thank you so much!" Said Peggy. "Here's one for you, Elizabeth." Elizabeth looked down at the package in her hand. She was again suddenly overwhelmed by the kindness of these strangers.
They had known her one day and yet it was as if they had known her a lifetime. She was not use to such kindness. With her, with her friends it had always been about what you could get for yourself, how this would help you get ahead. Every word, every thought, every action was weighed against profit or loss, position or place. She truly had nothing and yet it did not seem to matter with these people. They were kindness itself. She slowly opened the wrapping. Silent tears began to coarse down her cheeks as she looked at the polished black opal set in gold. She had never seen an opal with such fire. It was as if its very heart were smoldering. "You are too kind. I cannot accept this. I have nothing for you.

You do not know me. Why are you doing this?" All this came out in a rush between sobs as her voice cracked with the emotion. Neville smiled. "We do this because we are commanded to be kind. To do good, we might be entertaining angels without knowing it. Perhaps you are an angel, Miss Elizabeth." "No, not that, I'm not an angel. Quite the reverse." "Then, Miss Elizabeth, perhaps we do this because you are in need of help. Help is hard to take, isn't it. Grace is hard to accept. We want to work for what we get. We want what we think we deserve what we are owed. You are in need, Miss Elizabeth. Your child is in need. Please, allow us to help you.

You have come here in this time and in this place seeking death and yet you have found life, for yourself and for your baby.

Please allow us to give to you." Elizabeth's heart was conquered by the love that overflowed from these two strangers. She nodded. Neville and Peggy smiled. Neville continued to give out such small gifts as he and Peggy had found or made between them. Finally there came a large wooden case stamped Fortnum and Mason's from England. Peggy's eyes got bigger. She was excitement itself. "Well, Peggy, let's see what Uncle Rupert and Aunt Lettie have sent us shall we. I have no doubt it is filled with perfectly useless and expensive gifts sent with well-meaning ignorance of where we are and what we are doing." Neville took a small pry bar he used in the mine and pried open the box.

It was filled with those exactly expensive and useless things he had grown to expect from his only family. Pickled quail eggs. A Christmas pudding, long dried out. A woolen scarf, a fur hat and fur-lined leather gloves. Snow shoes. A tin of digestive biscuits. Tinned eels. Christmas crackers. The most foul smelling cheese any of them had ever encountered. With each successive package Neville handed them out in turn to the ladies and made a pile for himself. Elizabeth began to wonder if insanity ran in his family. Tinned boar. A mustache cup (Neville was clean shaven) a marble chess set with an onyx board.

Finally as the last of the packages had come out and everyone had stopped laughing from the hoard of useless items Elizabeth looked at Neville questioningly. "My Aunt and Uncle are quite old. They have been laboring under the delusion for years now, since I have come out here that I live in Antarctica, not Australia and that I am married with several small children. They send their equally ancient butler to Fortnum and Mason's, that venerable establishment with instructions to get things to help me survive in order to return to civilization which in their minds can only mean England, that green and pleasant land."

Neville was wiping his eyes from laughter. "It would be impossible to change their minds and so Peggy and I look on these gift boxes as a kind of glorious white elephant Christmas tradition.

We laugh because to do otherwise would just lead to frustration and perhaps even bitterness. Have a picked quail egg?" The morning had wandered toward noon. Elizabeth had taken Noel to her room to be fed changed and put down for a nap. Peggy had excused herself several times to see to luncheon. Elizabeth heard a tiny gong sound announcing lunch and she was met by Neville to escort her into the dining room, for so it was with a table and chairs of carved walnut. Silver settings, crystal stemware, and Ansley china. The two of them sat quietly while Peggy served and then sat down herself.
There was kangaroo; Elizabeth had tasted that before, but not as good as this, potatoes, parsnips, vegetables, even the pickled quail eggs had made it to the table, but not the eel Elizabeth was happy to see. She had not seen so much food at one time since the trip to Melbourne. She ate and ate. There had been small talk. Such talk as people who are strangers make to be polite, but finally Elizabeth could contain herself no longer. "Mr. Neville, I do not understand you or your situation. My late husband and I came here to seek a fortune we had lost. By the time we arrived we had almost nothing. I still have nothing and yet here you are surrounded by seeming wealth and yet you labor as hard as any coal miner. If you will forgive me, my curiosity has outpaced my manners, but would you please explain." "As you wish, Miss Elizabeth.

I come from an old English family with more land than money and very little sense. The things you see around you are family things passed down from generation to generation. I feel a certain responsibility to pass them on to such family as might come after me as those did who came before me, so I cannot bring myself to sell them.

Like you, I came to Australia to make my fortune, albeit with happier circumstances than you have found. I have made enough here to meet my needs, but not enough to return to England. The work is hard, but I am not afraid of work. It is only menial if I make it so.

I have a strong back to dig the stones and a quick mind that helps me make a profit. So, here we are surrounded by fine things eating with silver, china and crystal from days gone by. In the proverbial nutshell there you have it." Elizabeth nodded. "I too come from better circumstances; my father is a wealthy man. I grew up with fine things as did my husband, but he never learned to work believing that his family money would never run out. It did. We came here, but were swindled and lost everything. When you found me I had just buried my husband in a shallow grave I dug myself. I had determined to walk into the outback until I died from dehydration or sunstroke. Such little we had I gave to the local creditors to satisfy our debts and I am possessed of that in which Peggy found me and nothing more." "Your father? Could he help you? Would he help you?"

"That would require my asking and I would not wish to do so. While I possess little in this world's goods I have more than my share of pride." "Ah, yes, I understand pride quite well myself. I too possess a vast quantity of it." They continued the meal taking refuge in small talk once again. Peggy moved in and around them serving and eating with them. Finally she brought in the Christmas pudding. Neville poured brandy over it and set it on fire. Peggy had turned down the lamps so the flame would light the darkness. They marveled over the flame and the richness of the pudding. Each had their portion when the flames had died down and the lamp light blazed again. Elizabeth was savoring the rich flavors when she encountered something hard between her teeth. "Is there something in this cake?" She said with American directness. "Oh dear, yes, it's an old English tradition. I'm so sorry. I should have warned you." Elizabeth delicately captured the object in her serviette not wanting to cause a problem. "We put things in our Christmas puddings, for luck: coins, thimbles. I didn't have either so I gave Peggy something else to stir in the pudding. It's a gold nugget. Please forgive my negligence; on the other hand you are in possession now of more than what you came with. It's worth a good bit: enough to get you some clothes and a few necessities." Elizabeth's face colored slightly, but she smiled.

"I remember a story from my Sunday school days when the disciples found a coin in the mouth of a fish. Who am I to argue with such precedent?" They both laughed and Peggy smiled secretly to herself. She had made certain the nugget got in Elizabeth's pudding just as Mr. Neville had told her to do. The day continued on with more Christmas music on the victrola. Neville put on Handel's Messiah, that glorious piece. They spoke together. She cared for the baby. Neville treated her as a welcomed and expected guest. She retired early with Peggy sleeping in a chair in her room again. Again the feeding, the changing of the baby. Something that would be a part of her life now she was rapidly learning. The next morning Peggy brought her breakfast in her room. "Is Mr. Neville already at work in the mine?" "No, Miss Elizabeth, today is Boxing Day. No work today." "Is there going to be fighting?" Peggy giggled. "It's not that kind of boxing, Miss Elizabeth. I'll let Mr. Neville explain." They met again in the Drawing room. There was a radio playing giving the BBC news of the day. Civil unrest. Unemployment over 20% for Australia. Neville turned off the radio to save the batteries and wound up the victrola and put on more music. "Mr. Neville, what is Boxing Day? Peggy said I should ask you."

"Well, in England the people who cooked and served in the great houses never got Christmas day off and so Boxing Day is a sort of servant's holiday, but it was also a day when the poor box collections from the churches were distributed. So it became a day for doing good, visiting those in need. There are some miners I'd like to visit today who have fallen on hard times. Peggy and I usually go see some of them. Give away a few presents and generally do no work. You are welcome to join us or stay here as you wish. We won't be going far, but if you think it might be too taxing." "No, I think I'd like to go as long as I can take the baby and it won't be too hot." "Good. Peggy has your clothes cleaned and ready so you won't have to visit in my dressing gown. Australia's informal, but not quite that informal." And so they went out helping some, giving to others, just visiting with those who were lonely. Little Noel did very well, but by the end of the day, Elizabeth was weary. As they sat at tea that night, Neville spoke to Elizabeth. "Miss Elizabeth, I was wondering if you had a place to go, a place to live." "No, not really, we slept on the floor of the mine or in a small tent full of holes we found on a rubbish heap, but no, no place. I'm sure whatever little we had is gone by now, taken by scroungers." "Well, I'd like for you to consider staying here, working for me." Elizabeth's eyes widened and she began to draw herself up. "Please, no, nothing like that. Peggy has her own place, you would stay with her.

She has only been here these last two days because of you. No, you would stay with her and work." "What would you have me do? I have no skill that would be of use to you, except digging. I have learned to do that. Do you want me to dig for opals?" "No, but you do have a skill, an eye shall we say, for beauty. What I need is someone who can cut and polish the opals I find. I have the equipment. It's not hard work, but it needs an eye and I don't have it. I thought perhaps with your upbringing, your schooling, your style you would be able to get the best look out of the stones. You would cut and polish the stones, care for Noel and live with Peggy.

I would pay you a percentage of what we made on the stones if that would be amenable to you." Elizabeth was overcome. She truly had no thoughts beyond Noel's next feeding time. "I will show you what to do. You would work at your own pace. Think about it and let me know." "Is this another rescue, like Peggy? Are you saving me from myself?" "Do you need rescuing? Do you need saving?" "Yes, I believe I do. Thank you. I accept. When do I start?" "Whenever you feel up to it." said Neville. And so after a few more days of rest after giving birth and time spent buying some clothes and other needs with her gold nugget, Elizabeth began to polish opals. She was constantly amazed by their variety, their beauty, their color. Each day passed into the next. She chose the stones. Cut them and polished them. She fed Noel.

Peggy would watch him while Elizabeth worked. Noel grew, rolling over, crawling, feeding himself, taking his first wobbly steps. That was a momentous day. They all celebrated. Peggy was nanny, sister, friend, mother. Neville would send the stones to market when they were ready and pay her when the monies came in. In the evenings they would have tea together. Their lives wove in and around each other in the tapestry of daily life. They worked all day, listened to the radio after tea in the evenings. On Fridays they rolled up the carpets and danced to the ballroom sounds on the radio.

On Sundays Neville read a sermon from a Mr. Spurgeon or a Dr. Torrey. The days passed. The seasons changed. It was November again time for the Melbourne cup. They listened on the radio as White Nose won. December came in with the heat and the drought.

It was coming up to a year since Noel had been born, since Elizabeth had come to stay with Peggy. Each went about their daily task: Neville digging following a vein of opal, Elizabeth cutting and polishing the stones, Peggy cleaning, cooking, caring for everyone. Elizabeth was at the polishing wheel when Peggy rushed in Noel on her hip. "Miss Elizabeth, come quick, come quick. There's been a cave in. Mr. Neville's hurt bad." Elizabeth left everything and flew after Peggy. The dust from the cave-in filled the air. "Peggy, take Noel away from this. I'll see to Mr. Neville."

Neville was still breathing, but she could see blood. Slowly she began to clear the fallen stones away. She moved slowly, gently. She did not want to cause another cave-in or give Neville any pain. Finally when everything was cleared away she could begin to tend to Neville. He was still unconscious, but his breathing was steady. There was a gash on his head. His arm was at a strange angle. She straightened the arm gently, carefully. She cleaned his head and bound the wound. Slowly, painfully she dragged Neville away from the cave-in. With Peggy's help Elizabeth got Neville into his bed.

She left him there and went for the Doctor. As she scurried the events of last year came back to her. Last year she was walking away from life. Now she was walking for life, Neville's life. It welled up within her that she loved him. That she had loved him for some time, but love for her, true love, was a new feeling. One not easily trusted. As she strode along she began to weep and pray. She had never really prayed before. "Oh, God, please don't let Neville die. O, God, please don't let Neville die. I know you have no reason to listen to me. I am not your child. I do not know you, but Neville is yours. Please, don't let him die." As she prayed and walked and wept, her heart opened to God. The sermons she had heard Neville read the past year, the prayers she had hear him say, the words of her own father, the Sunday school lessons of her childhood all flooded her heart and mind.

In quiet desperation she fell to her knees and came to God as his child. She rose up and continued walking and praying. She reached the district clinic. The doctor was in. They rode back in his old Holden. He diagnosed a concussion. He set the broken arm. "Only time will heal him now," the doctor said. "Either he will come out of this on his own or he will never wake again. Keep him comfortable. I'll check back in a few days." And so the watch began. Day after day Elizabeth would work the mine, cut and polish the stones, doing Neville's work and her own.
At night she would sleep fitfully in a chair in his room watching over him. Peggy watched during the day. There was no change and it was coming on Christmas. The drought had continued. Water was low in the cisterns. Money was tight because Elizabeth had no idea how to sell what they had mined and no idea where Neville kept his money. Times continued to be hard for the nation, the world. Peggy had begun playing the Christmas records in the hopes that it would wake Neville. By now Elizabeth had almost given up hope. Every day she prayed that God would heal, that He would bring rain, that things would get better, but perhaps it was not God's will. Christmas Eve came and with it Noel's birthday. They celebrated quietly, Peggy making a small cake which Noel proceeded to smear all over his face. Even in this joy they were subdued. Peggy put Noel to bed and Elizabeth took up her lonely vigil over Neville.

In the small hours of Christmas morning Neville began to move, slowly at first restlessly, then his eyes opened. He looked confusedly about the room then his eyes lit on Elizabeth. "Elizabeth?" he whispered. "Yes."

Tears sprung to her eyes as she said it. "How long?" "Three weeks." "Cave- in?" "Yes." "Did you find it?" "Find what?" "The stone." "What stone?" "THE STONE. The biggest opal I have ever found." "No." "We've got to find it." He began pulling off the covers. She tried to stop him. "You can't. You're still weak." "Weak or not, we've got to find it."

He swung his legs around and began to get up. He lost his balance and began to fall. Elizabeth wrapped her arms around him. He kissed her full on the mouth. When they had parted she smiled and said, "You need a shave." "Whose fault is that? But I couldn't resist." Slowly, carefully by lamplight they made their way through the hall toward the mine. Neville was bewildered when they reached the place where he had been digging. "Where's the cave-in?" "Cleared away." "Who cleared it?" "I did. Mines don't dig themselves you know." He smiled at his words thrown back at him from a year ago. "But how?" "I shored up the mine. Dug what I could. I cleared the cave-in away. I cut and polished what I'd found. We kept going. There was nothing else to do." "We've got to find that stone. Where are the tailings?" "Up top."

They made their way to the surface where there was small shack and a mountain of tailings from the mine. "We'll never find it. I'm so sorry." As they reached the surface they heard and felt the first drops of rain. It was pouring, washing away the red dirt of the ages. After a time the downburst passed and in its place under the full moon shone opals, black and sparkling in the moonlight. Neville walked slowly over and picked up a stone larger than an egg and held it out to Elizabeth. "This is what I found. This is what caused the cave-in. I saw it in the vein. I was so excited I chiseled it out without thinking. Before I knew it the world fell on me. Just look at it. Even here in the moonlight you can see its fire." Elizabeth took the stone from him and turned it in her hand. She could indeed see its fire.

This would be the stone that would restore Neville's fortune. It was enormous; the reason people came to seek their fortune, to get a stake. Perhaps now he would leave Australia, leave her and go back to England, his home. "Now that you have this, what will you do?" She asked quietly putting the stone back in his hand. "Well, I was thinking of getting married if you'll have me. Will you marry me, Elizabeth?" She nodded, smiled and kissed him again. As they stood there in the moonlight surrounded by opals she told him what was in her heart, what had happened to her while he lay unconscious, of what God had done in her life. Finally she knew what Christmas was truly all about.

It was about the Christ Child, the Son of God, about family, about forgiveness, about healing the hurts of the heart. "Happy Christmas" Neville said. "Happy Christmas" Elizabeth smiled.

The End

6 CHRISTMAS 1944

The jeep ground its way through the heavy snow. The growl was swallowed by the snowy silence into a soft purr. The night wind whirled the snow from the ground at the three bodies huddled in the army's primary method of transport. They were lost. There had been an emergency surgery. They were headed back behind the ever changing lines of battle. All around them were the German units, the American 75th, the Canadians, the Brits, all locked in Hitler's desperate thrust to cut off supply lines. Around them was the Forest of Ardennes, in Belgium. Evergreens standing silent sentinel shrouded in snow. The windshield was down to keep the moon's reflection from betraying their position if any German flier was foolish enough to brave a night like this, but it was habit, the sergeant's habit whenever he drove the Major. Sergeant Hayes grasped the wheel like a vice, his eyes boring into the night ahead. The headlamps were off. The snow poured out its quietness like cream in the moonlight; the road a depression between the drifts.

Major Lambert sat stiffly beside the Sergeant, the Major's face wearing the constant scowl that had imprinted itself on him after the death of his wife and child.
His mind rolling the memory over and over played back in black and white like a newreel.
The blitz, the confusion, the destruction, the stumbling steps over the ruins of their house, seeking them, trying, hoping to find them miraculously alive in the chaos that had been their home.
He should have been with them. He should have protected them. He should have been able to save them. Would have saved them if there had been any life to save. He was the best surgeon in the army. He had saved life after life, limb after limb, of fliers, soldiers, sailors brought to his operating table there in London, but there was no life to save, only brokenness and death; his wife and child buried like discarded dolls in the wreckage. He had requested this field duty to get closer to the monsters who killed his family, a chance to fight back, just once. One year ago, tonight, Christmas Eve. For him Christmas wasn't presents and carols, Father Christmas, the Christ-Child, but death, destruction, blackness, loss.
Nurse Fiona Redgrave, Sister Redgrave, as the English call nurses, sat silently in the back wrapped in an army blanket and her thoughts. Through lashes flaked with blowing snow she looked lovingly at the Major.

She had come to love him quietly, know his pain in the last few months since being seconded to the American military's medical corps. She knew of his loss, like her own when she had returned from her stint in hospital to find a crater where her home and husband had been.

He had been on leave, an RAF pilot. She mourned his passing, but theirs had been a whirlwind romance driven by the war.

He had been sweet, charming, but as she had come painfully to know, not faithful. He was her husband, and now he was gone, his memory slowly slipping into time. There they rode, the Sergeant wrestling with the wheel, the Major, his soul, the Sister, her heart.

A sniper's bullet shattered the night, piercing the Sergeant's left shoulder spinning him out of the jeep. The Major and the Sister leaped from the rolling vehicle to the drift at the road's edge, instinctively the Major covering her with his body. The Sergeant, swearing under his breath, crawled to the jeep now embedded in the snow, its engine slowly rumbling in the night. He grabbed his M-1 from the back as another shot ricocheted off the hood. It was enough. He had seen the muzzle flash. He slid his carbine between the spokes of the steering wheel and emptied his magazine in the direction of the trees where the flash had come. He popped in another magazine and fired again. There was a scream, the crashing of branches, the scream continuing long after the echo of the firing had faded.

The Sergeant smiled as he slowly sank to his knees, his blood staining the snow. The jeep's engine coughed to a stop. Silence flooded in except for the fading moan of the German sniper and the whisper of the wind under a moon half grown. The Major, crouching, made his way to the Sergeant. He deftly peeled back his layers of uniform, sprinkled the sulfa powder and pressed a bandage into the wound front and back and slid the needle filled with morphine into the sergeant. "Nurse, nurse, hold this bandage.
I'm going to finish what the Sergeant started." Thoughts whirled through Fiona's mind as she crawled to the wounded man. "You have taken an oath, Doctor 'To do no harm.' How can you think of killing that man?" "How? Because he killed my wife and son and thousands of others." "Not him, Doctor. . . . Hitler yes, the Generals yes, faceless men from the sky, but not him." She spoke these words with an intensity he had never heard in her voice. Even as she spoke them she pressed the bandage into the Sergeant's shoulder. "Very well, Sister! I have taken an oath to do no harm, but I don't have to do him any good either. Leave him; he'll die soon enough anyway with the loss of blood and the cold. Right now we've got to figure a way to get out of here before we join him." Through the snow covered night they could see the lights of a house nearby. They could smell the smoke from the chimney. Strangely they could hear music, drifting on the air. It was Handel's Messiah, the Hallelujah Chorus.

Christmas Time

The Major muscled the Sergeant onto his shoulder; Sister grabbed the carbine and the Doctor's bag. Slowly they trudged through the snow to the farmhouse. A dog began to bark.

As they drew near, light spilled from the doorway along with the familiar music from an ancient Victrola. A sturdy man carrying an aged, but menacing shotgun filled the open door. "Comme qui dirait? Who goes there?" "Nous sommes Americans, we are Americans. One of us is wounded. May we enter? The French coming easily from Sister Redgrave's mouth. "Entrée, Enter, I speak ze English, come, come and be warm," the farmer said. They stepped into Christmas, not a New York Christmas, not a London Christmas, but Christmas. Golden lamplight filled the air with warmth, comfort. A fire danced in the hearth. There by the fire in a wooden rocker sat a very pregnant young lady. "Zis is my daughter, Eugenie. I am Henri. On such a night you are welcome. Bring your man in here." In a small bedroom off the room in which they stood dripping melting snow they laid the Sergeant gently down. A small hiss escaped his lips as he touched the mattress. Sister began to remove his boots and ease him out of his heavy parka. She covered him with a quilt at the foot of the bed. Silently the Major watched her as she moved with the gentle efficiency of one used to such things, but he also saw the warmth in her eyes. She cared.

He was long past caring for his patients; his only worry was to do a good job, to succeed at his work, to fix the problem, defeat the Germans. "Monsieur," The farmer broke his reverie. "Je suis une L'Doctor. I am a Doctor." the Major said. "Bon, good," Henri answered. "We may need a doctor. Eugenie's time is very near." "I'm not that kind of. . . . It's been a long time since. . . .I. . . . "His words faltered. The last baby he had delivered was his own son. Smiling he had placed him on his wife's breast. She had smiled through the sweat glowing on her face and kissed him, pulling the covers up to warm the infant. "We will be honored to do what we can." Sister had spoken, coming around him in the small doorway. "There is another wounded man in the edge of the wood." "No! Leave him!" barked the Major. "He is a German, the Boshe, he shot my sergeant. He is the enemy!" "No," spoke Sister Redgrave quietly, "He is wounded, he is a patient." "Tonight is a night for life, not death." the farmer said. "I will find him. I will bring him." As the farmer put on his coat and made his way out into the snow, the Major whirled on Sister Redgrave. "You can't honestly expect me to operate on him, to save him. I hope I can save the Sergeant's arm, his life, but this German." "Doctor, you must! Saving lives is what you do. I have never seen anyone, any surgeon, as skilled as you. I have seen you work.

I have seen you save limbs, literally bring these broken men back from the brink of death with an urgency that must be driven by caring." "No. I stopped caring long ago. I work as I do because I want to defeat what the enemy seeks to destroy. I work as I do because I don't want to fail.

I am driven by my hatred of the Nazis and my desire to succeed. How can you expect me to save a life that has sought to destroy mine? How can you think I can operate on this man, forgive this man." "Doctor, you can start by forgiving yourself. Forgive yourself that you couldn't save your wife and child. That you somehow should have prevented their deaths. That it is not your fault. Forgive yourself, then you can forgive him." The words were out now and she could not bring them back.

The farmer burst through the door struggling with the limp body on his shoulder. "Vite, Vite, clear the table!" The Sister and Eugenie quickly removed the plates and mugs from the table. "Leave the cloth." The farmer said.

He moved to the end of the long farm table, gently rolling the soldier from his shoulder onto the cloth and then moving around to slide him further up the table until the body was laying full length. "Can you help him? Monsieur L'Doctor? Can you save him?" The farmer's deep voice rumbled. Even as he spoke Eugenie and the Sister began to ease the soldier out of the white covering that hid him in the snow.

The Sister with quick deft hands, Eugenie moving slowly, but carefully. "Il est si jeune" spoke Eugenie. He is so young." He is only a boy" whispered the Sister. It was true. Here before them lay a youth of eighteen, perhaps nineteen: the white, nearly invisible brush of his first mustache curling above his lips. Lambert had heard that the Germans were using boys of 15, 16, 17. "He is a sniper! He is the enemy." Growled the Doctor. As the Sister began to assess the boy's wounds the farmer reasoned with the doctor. "Mon ami, here is zis boy. It is Christmas. It is the time we celebrate the birth of the Holy One, the Christ Child. For centuries men have fought and died in war, but on tzis night, zis Holy night they have made peace. Can you not find it in your heart to do zis thing tonight? I do not know what bitterness has filled your heart, what sorrow, but it will overcome you if you do not let it go. The Germans, they killed my Eugenie's husband, he was no older than this boy. They have robbed my grandchild of his father. They have ravaged our land, but I know if I do not forgive I will be no better than the worst of them.

'Forgive us our trespasses as we forgive those who trespass against us' that is what the Holy Book says. That is what our Savior whose birth we celebrate zis night said to those who follow him." In an instant the memories of childhood flooded back through the Doctor's mind; his mother's soft reading from the Bible.

Sunday school lessons. Then the services he had attended with his wife held in homes and church shelters during the bombings. He nodded to Sister and began to prepare for the surgery. The Sister had given the boy morphine.

The Doctor looked at this boy wrapped in the blood spattered uniform of the enemy; the ravages of the bullets, a shoulder wound, another in his upper thigh, those were simple enough and would heal, but in his right eye was a splinter of wood from a tree struck by one of the bullets. He would lose the eye.

Quickly, feverishly he began to work, extracting bullets, repairing the wounds; the farmer bringing supplies from the jeep, plasma, thread, sulfa. Sister wiping the sweat from his forehead, handing him the instruments, staunching bleeds. The eye was the most difficult. It could not be saved. It took hours. When the final stitch was done, the bandages in place the Doctor turned to his sergeant, repairing and closing his shoulder wound. A great weariness flooded over the Doctor as he washed his hands after the surgeries. Sister Redgrave smiled wanly. Henri had emptied buckets, boiled water, fetched and carried stood in attendance. It was midnight.

Eugenie had long since climbed the narrow stairs to her bed. Now there was only the crackling of the Yule log in the stone fireplace, a soft hissing of escaping moisture. "Something to eat?" Henri asked. "Some bread and cheese, perhaps some hot chocolate?"

Sister Redgrave smiled, "That would be nice."
"And you Doctor? Would you like something?"
At that moment, Eugenie's scream caught them up in a gasping jump. Into the fatigue that comes when an exhausting job is finished dropped the adrenalin rush of another crisis that must be faced. The baby was coming. The Major and the Sister raced up the stairs to see Eugenie's mouth soundlessly screaming, her eyes bulging, the pain intense. A brief examination told the Doctor all he needed to know. The child was breach, turned sideways in the womb. This was not going to be an easy birth. He began to try to manipulate the baby, to turn it head down in the womb. Slowly, agonizingly the baby moved between contractions that wracked Eugenie's thin body. Exhaustion was beginning to set in with her and the Doctor. Again the hot water, again the clean sheets, again the blood staining the snow white cotton. Slowly the baby began to emerge. The head, the shoulders, then all at once he made an appearance. The cord was cut; the baby swaddled and placed on Eugenie's breast, just like his own child, his own wife. Eugenie smiling weakly, the baby crying softly and tears coursing down the Doctor's face as well. It had all come back to him in the suddenness of birth itself. His wife, his child, his loss, his love. Christmas, the child Christ, his Faith.
This child, this birth, this night had brought back his life, his love. As he turned away, Nurse Redgrave gently took him in her arms.

He held her fiercely, tightly as if she would evaporate. "I'm here. It's all right. I understand." She whispered through her own tears. The love that the Doctor had hidden in his heart for her poured out with the grief, the pain, the release all at once in wave of emotion from his frozen heart. Bewildered, Eugenie stared. Henri's faced brightened in an instant of comprehension. "Soyez amoureux, they are in love. Something terrible happened to him and now it is healed. You have healed him Eugenie, you and your baby and this night." "Comme vous appelez vous?" "Doctor, she wants to know your name, and I confess so do I." translated Sister. "Michael, I am Michael, Je suis Michael." "Zen we shall call him Michel, Michel Noelle. Michel for you and Noelle for the night, yes." smiled Eugenie. "A good name, a good night! What is it you English say, 'Happy Christmas' Joyeax Noelle! Eugenie, you rest. I will see to our guests." Slowly, happily they made their way down the stairs to the great room of the farmhouse. But in the midst of the joy and the peace lay the German soldier, like a great weight that smothered them. What to do with him? "Sleep now, Monsieur L' Doctor, and you as well, Ma Soeur, I will look over everyone. It will be like lambing season, yes."

Fiona collapsed on Henri's bed in the back room. The Doctor fell asleep in a chair by the Sergeant. Henri wandered about checking, dozing in a chair by the fire, occasionally stirring the blaze, keeping it warm.

The dawn came slowly, beautifully glowing over the snow covered trees and falling in strong shafts on the sleepers in the farmhouse. Henri woke to the sound of the baby's soft cry for food. The farmer made his morning rounds; gathered eggs, milked the cows, fed the pigs, all the chores he did every day of his life. Then he went back into the farmhouse and made preparation to feed his other charges. Each woke slowly to the smell of bacon, strong Belgian coffee and baking bread.
The Doctor checking on his patients. Nurse Redgrave doing what she could to make herself as presentable as possible. They met before the fire touching in the small ways of shy lovers. The three ate by the fire on small trays perched on their laps. Enjoying the coffee and the fresh eggs as only those who have been deprived of such things can do. They made conversation as strangers when some shared catastrophe has brought them together, slowly feeling their way along in two languages. Into this desultory silence whispered the German, "Vasser." They had almost forgotten him. Now Sister Redgrave's training asserted itself again. Now she knew her place in this little world. She quickly got some water and pressed it to the wounded boy's lips, a slow smile crept into his face. "Danke" "You're welcome," Sister replied automatically and then a look of fear and dismay swept over the bandaged face of the young soldier.

"Sprectenzie Anglander?" "Ya." "Well, that's good, because I don't think my German is up to the task. You remember last night? Shooting?" "Ya. Americaner, jeep, ya. On purpose I miss." The Major was on his feet, "What? You shot my sergeant!" "Ya, yes, but not to kill, only to vound, ya? I am German sniper. I do not miss, but is Christmas. I do not kill, only vound. Besides, he shoot me too, yes?" "Yes, the Sergeant shot you too." whispered Sister. "Mine eye?" "Gone. I could not save it. There was a shard from the tree. You understand this?"

"Ya." spoke the youth, a smile curling around his lips. "Why do you smile?" spoke the Sister softly. "With one eye, no sniper, no shoot, no killings." said the young soldier very matter of factly. "I live. That is enough." Slowly the young man began to tell his story. His family had watched as the Jews were rounded up. Then the others; cripples, the simple, then finally the Gestapo had come for his family, true believers in Jesus Christ. Because of his youth he had been taken into the army, trained as a sniper. "I miss a lot of shootings, only vound." He did not know where his family was. He thought perhaps dead like the others who disappeared into the KZs, the concentration camps. "I zink I will not fight anymore." "You are my prisoner!" Henri spoke these words harshly. "I captured you in the wood. I brought you here. You are my prisoner. I will decide what you will do and not do."

These words fell like lead into the warmth of Christmas day. "Surely we must get him to a hospital?" said Sister Redgrave. "Or at least as a prisoner of war in England." followed the Major.
The young German's face was a mask of white. "He is my prisoner, and I will keep him here, nursing him until he is better, and when he is better he will work here on the farm, this farm so far from the war and the battles and the Germans who have been pushed back by the Americans. And perhaps when I am working on the farm, Eugenie can guard him while she cares for her child."
A smile slowly spread itself over Henri's face and the color returned to the young man. "Zat only seems to be right, Herr Henri. I am content to be your prisoner and perhaps, although I have not seen her, I will be Eugenie's prisoner as well?" "Perhaps." purred Henri. Later the Sergeant woke, feeling his wound, but thirsty and hungry when he smelled the bacon still on the air. The day, Christmas Day passed in a slow dream for all of them. Eugenie awoke and nursed the baby. She came down the stairs slowly holding him swaddled in her arms. The young German, whose name they learned was Wilhelm, blushed when he saw how lovely she was. The Doctor and Sister Redgrave went for a walk and returned smiling, holding hands, glowing with joy, the Doctor calling her Fiona. The patients slept and woke, ate and slept again. The sleep bringing the healing they needed.

Henri continued to be the host and the farmer.

In the evening, he read from the book of Luke, chapter 2; the story of the Christ child. 1 ¶ And it came to pass in those days, that there went out a decree from Caesar Augustus, that all the world should be taxed.

2 (*And* this taxing was first made when Cyrenius was governor of Syria.)

3 And all went to be taxed, every one into his own city.

4 And Joseph also went up from Galilee, out of the city of Nazareth, into Judaea, unto the city of David, which is called Bethlehem; (because he was of the house and lineage of David:)

5 To be taxed with Mary his espoused wife, being great with child.

6 And so it was, that, while they were there, the days were accomplished that she should be delivered.

7 And she brought forth her firstborn son, and wrapped him in swaddling clothes, and laid him in a manger; because there was no room for them in the inn.

8 ¶ And there were in the same country shepherds abiding in the field, keeping watch over their flock by night.

9 And, lo, the angel of the Lord came upon them, and the glory of the Lord shone round about them: and they were sore afraid.

10 And the angel said unto them, Fear not: for, behold, I bring you good tidings of great joy, which shall be to all people.

11 For unto you is born this day in the city of David a Saviour, which is Christ the Lord.

12 And this *shall be* a sign unto you; Ye shall find the babe wrapped in swaddling clothes, lying in a manger.

13 And suddenly there was with the angel a multitude of the heavenly host praising God, and saying,

14 Glory to God in the highest, and on earth peace, good will toward men.

15 And it came to pass, as the angels were gone away from them into heaven, the shepherds said one to another, Let us now go even unto Bethlehem, and see this thing which is come to pass, which the Lord hath made known unto us.
16 And they came with haste, and found Mary, and Joseph, and the babe lying in a manger.
17 And when they had seen *it*, they made known abroad the saying which was told them concerning this child.
18 And all they that heard *it* wondered at those things which were told them by the shepherds.
19 But Mary kept all these things, and pondered *them* in her heart.
20 And the shepherds returned, glorifying and praising God for all the things that they had heard and seen, as it was told unto them.
21 ¶ And when eight days were accomplished for the circumcising of the child, his name was called JESUS, which was so named of the angel before he was conceived in the womb.
22 And when the days of her purification according to the law of Moses were accomplished, they brought him to Jerusalem, to present *him* to the Lord;
23 (As it is written in the law of the Lord, Every male that openeth the womb shall be called holy to the Lord;)
24 And to offer a sacrifice according to that which is said in the law of the Lord, A pair of turtledoves, or two young pigeons.
25 ¶ And, behold, there was a man in Jerusalem, whose name *was* Simeon; and the same man *was* just and devout, waiting for the consolation of Israel: and the Holy Ghost was upon him.
26 And it was revealed unto him by the Holy Ghost, that he should not see death, before he had seen the Lord's Christ.
27 And he came by the Spirit into the temple: and when the parents brought in the child Jesus, to do for him after

the custom of the law,

28 Then took he him up in his arms, and blessed God, and said,

29 Lord, now lettest thou thy servant depart in peace, according to thy word:

30 For mine eyes have seen thy salvation,

31 Which thou hast prepared before the face of all people;

32 A light to lighten the Gentiles, and the glory of thy people Israel.

33 And Joseph and his mother marvelled at those things which were spoken of him.

34 And Simeon blessed them, and said unto Mary his mother, Behold, this *child* is set for the fall and rising again of many in Israel; and for a sign which shall be spoken against;

35 (Yea, a sword shall pierce through thy own soul also,) that the thoughts of many hearts may be revealed.

Henri finished the reading and closed the Bible. Silence reigned for a moment as the truth of the scripture filled the farmhouse.

They sang carols, "Silent Night" the young soldier echoing "Stil Nacht" in his native tongue. Henri put a Christmas record on the Victrola and wound it up. They exchanged such presents as they had about them. Chocolates, needles, thread, a handkerchief for Eugenie from the Sister, a surprising number of stockings from the Sergeant's pack. "Well, you never know." He said sheepishly. The Doctor brought out a gold watch on a chain that he gave to Henri for young Michel.

Even the young German after whispering to Sister Redgrave, who fetched it from his kit, made his offering, a wooden carving of the Nativity and a gold necklace set with a garnet. "Pour vous, for you, Mademoiselle, it was my Maters, my mothers."

The days passed slowly as the Sergeant became strong enough to move. The jeep had long since been driven to a shed on the farm safe from prying eyes. Finally the day came when Lambert felt his sergeant could safely brave the cold and the ride without harm. They embraced Henri and Eugenie. Kissed the baby.

The Doctor took one last look at his now cocky German patient whose young, strong body was healing rapidly and pronounced him well on his way to recovery.

It was long after the first of the year when they made their way back to American lines with careful directions from Henri.

Henri waved and smiled as he watched the jeep drive away, the sergeant on a stretcher on the back; the lovely Sister with her hand on the Doctor's shoulder as he maneuvered the drifts on the road. Henri smiled with the knowledge that once again a child born at Christmas had changed everything.

THE END.

Doug Whitley is a husband, a father, an actor, a playwright, an author. He travels the world portraying characters from the Bible and preachers from history. You can reach him at www.preachersofthepast.com

can't believe how beautiful this place is. You had totally forgotten! Tears fall from your eyes, you are ecstatic and utterly astonished. You wonder to yourself how you could have ever left this place; it's the most amazing place ever!

You had to leave your home, and only after experiencing the "outside" world did you come back and experience home yet again—but this time in total awe. Nothing changed—it's the same home, the same Bora Bora, but since that was all you knew back then—you weren't aware of how sublime it really was. Now you are in bliss.

This is just a little metaphorical story. It shouldn't be taken at face value. If primordial awareness hadn't illusorily separated itself so that it could experience the awakening to its existence and the enlightening return to itself, it would have never known how Godly it was[25]. It ever was, is, and will be absolutely divine and One, but without knowing it. Unless one tastes separateness and form—how can unity and formlessness exist?

---

[25] It is sometimes said that the return of the individual consciousness toward its absolute source is an enrichment in comparison to when it left. Yet this can only be said to be true from the dual perspective, for from the non-dual absolute one, besides no movement having ever occurred, nothing could improve or add anything to what already is beyond perfection and completeness. Duality, change, and evolution happen without ever happening—what a beautiful paradox!

The perceived duality of manifested form and the non-perceptible unmanifested nothingness are actually one and the same Reality. Through the ego-mind, one perceives form and divisiveness; through pure awareness, one "perceives" formless unity only.

Eventually all sentient beings will have to look within themselves, find that common unmanifested source and consciously come back to it. You, just like the Universe, go through a cycle of creation (the birth of "I"), expansion (the beginning of life up until one's body starts declining), dissolution (the end of life, up until one's body dies), and then withdraw back to the unmanifested (death).

This cycle repeats itself infinitely, unless or until one realizes his/her inherent eternity as the primordial consciousness. It also occurs every day through the cycles of waking up (creation), wakefulness with fresh energy (expansion—until the peak of daily energy), wakefulness with low energy (dissolution—from the beginning of declining energy until you fall asleep) and death (deep dreamless sleep).

So too, will the universe itself withdraw back to its original unmanifested singularity after trillions of years of outward expansion.

Sooner or later, we have to know our source. Many decide

to seek it only when they enter into a cycle of dissolution (the so-called *Sannyasa* stage of life within the Hindu philosophy of the four *ashramas*). In this cycle, the body isn't as strong and healthy as it used to be, one has already lived outwardly directed toward the world, experienced its pains and pleasures, and then starts to become less and less identified with the ego and forms. This is indeed a great opportunity, but most people shy away from such self-discovery especially since it's not encouraged in society. There are many taboos in society, and the subject of death is certainly one of them. One is discouraged from thinking about, discussing, or even discovering what death is and what happens when we die.

This great opportunity to embrace and discover the consciousness that survives the dissolution of the body is thus typically wasted. When death comes, the majority of people are either drugged up, barely conscious, or suffering from a great deal of fear, anxiety and regret.

You can change that. It doesn't matter whether you are already in the dissolution phase of life or not. Regardless of all that, you have the now. Now is the time to sincerely start discovering the timeless. Now is actually the only "time" that truly exists. It never began and it will never end. It is not even correct to call it time, because time doesn't contain the now; the ever-present now contains time.

You will not survive forever. A time will come when you have to embrace death. Resisting it will do no good because death will come whether we want it or not. Nobody has survived forever—only nothing survives forever, and that's why you must find the nothingness within you, as you, for then you are eternal life itself.

CHAPTER 17
A SIMPLE TRADE-OFF

Just like in economics, the path toward enlightenment has a trade-off. You will have to trade-off a common life for one dedicated to the Truth, to the Divine, to unravel the ultimate mysteries of existence, to unravel your true Self.

Rather than spending countless hours watching TV, playing video games, reading novels, and just wasting time in general, you have to apply that free time to your journey. This trade-off is easily seen as non-problematic once you realize that you are not being asked to choose between two great things: you are being asked to throw away the garbage that you've been feeding your mind and replace it with mindfulness, wisdom, joy, peace, awareness, and love. Is that a trade-off?

The real trade-off comes when you have to choose between your identity as a person, as "I am so and so," and the egoless impersonal Beingness. It is not so hard, though the ego makes it seem that way.

Since the cost of something is what you give up to get it, one might wonder: "What do I have to give up to achieve enlightenment?"

You give up the one who gives up—the "I-ego." That is all.

It is the most expensive thing ever though, because giving up "I" is giving up everything. However, the benefit of giving up "I" is unfathomable timelessness. You give up the temporary to be everlasting. This doesn't sound that bad, does it?

The "I-ego" fears that if it stops the thinking process altogether, it will cease to exist or, at best, become dull or bored. However, dullness and boredom are simply consequences of not being satisfied with the present moment. Why is the "I-ego" not satisfied with the present moment? Because it is so accustomed to showing interest in thoughts and mental contents (of the past and future)—and therefore feeding them—that when they are not present, it becomes increasingly frustrated.

When one remains simply "just Being," unified with silence, one shifts the focus from the mind's contents to its substratum, empty consciousness. Eventually, consciousness' intoxicating fragrance will prove to be far more interesting than any thought or mental content could ever be. It will bathe you in happiness.

This pure happiness is all-encompassing, a memorable fragrance of Being. Its presence liquefies even the hardest rock, turning it into a jovial freshness. Happiness is not just a byproduct of Being—it is Being itself! They are one and the same.

Being can't really be understood, because prior to understanding, it already IS. It can't even be experienced because it is also prior to experience! Being is primordially without a subject or object.

In this world, doing is overlapped into Being, but they don't have to negate each other. The sun simply is (beingness). However, the sun also warms up the planet, gifts it with days and nights and gives life to Earth (doing). Can you see how the sun's doing is also Being? That's how a truly enlightened human acts—as the sun.

With enlightenment, doing melts into Being, because there is no individual agent of action or doer. Such identification has already been seen through.

Being, like the sun shining down lightly on one's face during sunrise, is unconditional, gentle, sweet, and it emanates a natural softness and love; but Being is also all-powerful, just like the sun is—capable of wiping out entire planets and incinerating anything that is thrown into it.

Enlightenment does make a human the most powerful being in the Universe, but not in the conventional sense. You might not visibly change the world, although some Masters did. You might not become well-known, although some Masters did. You might not become wealthy, although some Masters did. You might not have any supernatural abilities, although some Masters did[26]. You might not have any students, although many Masters did. You might receive no recognition whatsoever in your lifetime for your massive direct or indirect contributions to humanity, although most Masters did. Society might think you are a simpleton, a nobody.

Being nobody is generally so puzzling to the mind that it wastes no time starting to fill up that empty space of Being. The mind cannot endure being nothing and nobody! However, if you fill yourself with an identity, with a personality, then you are clouding your own awareness of Being. Being nothing is true freedom; only when you are not filled with concepts, thoughts and impressions are you free to be filled with the eternal love of God.

Ashtavakra, the revered Vedic sage, was ridiculed for being

---

[26] See *Siddhis* in the Glossary.

handicapped; Jesus Christ was crucified; Ramana Maharshi was poisoned and beaten up. What will happen to you in the course of your life? Nobody knows. Your life doesn't even belong to you, so why are you still claiming it? Life belongs to Life, not to any individual consciousness.

Are you afraid? You don't need to be; you will not be "you" anymore after realizing who you truly are. The limited "you" who you think you are is a short concocted story; it is fake. The real "you"—infinity itself—is one with Ashtavakra, Jesus Christ and Ramana Maharshi. The real "you" is one with Life.

CHAPTER 18

DECODING THE GOD STATE

The nature of our consciousness is happiness. As we live under the rule of the ego-mind, our apparent nature is seeking happiness (which can also be termed restlessness). To realize our true nature, we have to realize who we are. Rather than being identified with the contents of our mind, we realize the pure subjectivity of being.

After realizing that our nature is one of happiness—which means *it is happiness itself*—we are in a permanent state of happiness, because we are happiness itself. Turiya is just the integration of this permanent state of happiness more and more into our life.

As may be obvious, if we are in a constant yet smooth state of happiness, we live our lives with tremendous peace as well, because nobody is truly happy if they are not at peace. Anyone who is at peace is also happy; therefore, peace equals happiness. Hence we can say that the relative manifestation of Self-Realization is the integration and assimilation of constant peace and happiness into our lives.

Peace and happiness equal completeness. If we are at peace and fully happy, then we are truly complete—nothing lacks, and there's nothing we desire because this moment is enough. Now is enough. We accept life as it is, rather than rejecting it.

If peace, happiness, and completeness are the same, then we are in a state of love as well. When we are in a moment of pure love, we are at peace, happy and complete. When we are in a state of love, peace, happiness, and completeness, we seem to temporarily shrink or even lose the imagined boundaries that we have put around ourselves. With no boundaries, we are not experiencing a moment—*we are one with the moment.*

We can't be one and two at the same time; hence when we are absorbed in the happiness of being in the present moment, we are actually experiencing life through that angle of perception within the whole universe. We are the unified universal being, manifesting life in a state of conscious unity within the capable limits of our pure mind.

When we are One, spontaneous universal wisdom manifests

through our pure mind as well. There is no knowledge the Whole doesn't possess.

Happiness, peace, completeness, love, wholeness, wisdom—the permanent integration of these into our life is the hallmark of the God State, Turiya. These "fragrances" of God are not new "qualities," they are merely the intrinsic qualities of our true nature infusing our objective experience in both the waking and dream state.

If the integration is too strong ("remaining" in level 4 for too long), our mind—no matter how pure it is (as the "Transcendental-I")—can't hold the life-force in the body and it disperses to universality, possibly leading to physical death. No physical life can sustain the pure cosmic bliss of God in its full force—only the subjective universality can.

Your level of Turiya integration will always be proportional to how much happiness, peace, completeness, love, wholeness, and wisdom—which are not six different things, but one only—permeate and emanate from your divine life.

Turiya is the celebration of life!

CHAPTER 19

MEET DARKNESS

Darkness. What is darkness?

Darkness is more mysterious than light. Light is welcoming, Light is warm, Light loves, Light embraces.

But darkness? Darkness is unknown.

Darkness is not bad. We're way beyond those dichotomies of Maya.

Darkness is all around life. It surrounds life like the abyss of the unknown. You encounter darkness every time you fall into deep dreamless sleep. You will meet it again when your body passes away.

Darkness is ignorance. That ignorance surrounds your life; that ignorance meets you in the unconsciousness of sleep; that ignorance will meet you at death.

But what if you meditate on darkness?

Stop.

Really, stop now. Stop for a moment. Don't let this moment be just one of those moments that unknowingly passes by in the blink of an eye. Don't let your life be a glimpse. Life surrounded by ignorance will always be a glimpse. Life surrounded by darkness will always be a glimpse.

Stop.

. . .

Ok. Now that I've got your attention, there's something I want to tell you.

Yes, to you. You only, and to nobody else.

Darkness doesn't exist. Ignorance doesn't exist. They are merely the absence of Light—the absence of the Light of Awareness.

Humankind seeks to lengthen their life-span so that they can earn more, accumulate more, and so on. Everybody is in a hurry, trying to live as much as possible, trying to pack their schedules, squeezing every little thing into every available second. But what do they earn? What do they accumulate? An extended period of suffering?

We all go through our lives without ever stopping.

Whatever you are thinking about right now—just stop.

There comes a time in our lives where we inevitably have to stop. Not stopping will lead to burnout, depression or possibly even death.

Stop.

. . .

For a moment, watch your breath. See how beautifully it comes in, and how it peacefully goes out. It's the majestic rhythm of life, often overlooked.

DO NOT SKIP AHEAD. *Really watch your breath*. Keep watching it. Slowly, steadily and effortlessly, just watch it for a moment.

Whenever you exhale, let all the weight drop. Notice that you not only feel better, but also how everything seems to slow down. Keep doing this for a couple of minutes. Let your guard down.

. . .

When something as simple as watching the breath can bring such relaxation and peace, imagine what discovering the inner treasure that we all have can bring.

It can enlighten all the ignorance—all the darkness.

It is time to enlighten darkness with the sun within. Darkness has no power; ignorance has no power. Darkness is the absence of Light. How can it have any power? Only if you are scared of it.

You are scared of it because you've met it before, many times. It is present at the time of death. It is like death. Darkness unconsciously reminds you of death.

Find the inner Light, and darkness will be revealed to be Light itself. You cannot attack, harm, damage or destroy darkness—but you can enlighten it.

Why then do you keep looking outside yourself, looking for materialistic stuff, money, possessions, power, status, worldly success, perfect relationships, perfect body, objective knowledge, and so on?

What are you doing with your life?

You have all that you need already in you. This is not a philosophical or "New Age" statement. It's really the truth, but one that you must find and realize by yourself, in yourself.

The Self will remember what it has never forgotten.

Most people are born to die, and vice versa. But you?

You are born to live forever.

CHAPTER 20

WAKE UP NOW

The spiritual path is not a straightforward journey. Life will hit you hard and drop you to your knees—so that you can rise up again and realize that you're not even the one living life. Life is living itself, impersonally. We get so attached to the convincing illusion that it is "I" who is living it, that we get lost in the sense of being the doer and performer of actions. It's as if a cell thought it was living its own life.

Listen to me now:

You are truly special.

Not your personality; not your ideas; not your opinions; no, none of that. Those are not special. You are special. No practice or anything is special. You are special, your very own awareness which is who you are. Everything else needs your awareness to make itself present to you. Everything needs awareness to exist and to be. You will never be able to know or experience whether anything exists without your awareness of it, because you can only know with awareness! Yet awareness is present even if nothing else is. You don't need anything to be present. Thus your awareness is the source of everything. You are indeed special.

This specialness can't be possessed by the ego, just like a candle can't possess the sun. This specialness is the essence out of which even the ego is made. This specialness is home. Your awareness is your own home.

Don't attempt to obtain security if it costs you your peace of mind. That is the slogan of everybody's life, and it sums it up quite well. And even so, that security is but an illusion—it's not true. Tomorrow you might be dead or diagnosed with cancer, or you might be fired from your job, your house might burn down, or you may be robbed of your money. Where's the security in that? There's no security in this world.

True security is walking with no ground and knowing that you won't fall. Because even if you fall, God will catch you.

I have often been asked what the name SantataGamana means. Santata means "Continuous" or "Unbroken" and Gamana, "Togetherness," "Oneness" or "Union."

SantataGamana means *Unbroken Oneness*.

Imagine that you are taking your last breath, and you have in front of you all of your possessions, money, goals, ideologies, mundane accomplishments, etc.

Do they seem important now?

All of your problems... do they seem like an issue now?

Even your loved ones. You have to let go of them. It's okay. What you love about them is not their body, and it's not even their personality. What they love about you, whether they know it or not, is not your body or personality either. What you love in them and they in you is that Love which is *deathless*, beyond the concept of love. And you are not leaving behind or saying goodbye to that Love. You are actually going to merge and dissolve in it. You are actually going to recognize that you are indeed that very Love.

You are not saying goodbye, but on the contrary, you are actually going to finally be one with that eternal Love.

If you knew that you were going to die in about one minute, what would instantly lose all meaning? All of those things that suddenly stopped mattering, discard them immediately. They can't stand the sword of pure discernment.

Let go. Don't look back. Don't hold anything back. Let the pull of pure awareness pull you back toward itself.

Now you don't have to wait until your body dies to be one with this infinite Love. You can do it while still living. This book, along with the previous ones in this series, shows you the way. The way your Heart has been telling you all of this time.

It's time you are One.

It's time you are Unbroken Oneness.

It's time you yourself are... SantataGamana.

Thank you for taking this journey with me.

I want to leave here my heartfelt gratitude to you for having read this book. I hope that it has helped you in your journey toward the truth of who you are. If you've enjoyed reading this book or any of the other books in the *Real Yoga Series*, please consider showing your support by leaving a review on the Amazon page.

These reviews have been essential in helping take these books toward more genuine seekers, many of whom have contacted me throughout these months, not only to clarify their doubts but to share profound and beautiful words. Leaving a review really makes a difference.

Subscribe and receive the ebook **Uncovering the Real** plus updates and information regarding new books or articles, which will be sent about once or twice a month.

www.RealYoga.info

If you have any doubts or questions regarding this or any of the other books, feel free to contact me at:

Santata@RealYoga.info

Read also, by the same author of *Turiya - The God State*:

— KRIYA YOGA EXPOSED

The Truth About Current Kriya Yoga Gurus & Organizations.
Going Beyond Kriya, Contains the Explanation of a Special Technique Never Revealed Before in Kriya Literature.

— THE SECRET POWER OF KRIYA YOGA

Revealing the Fastest Path to Enlightenment.
How Fusing Bhakti & Jnana Yoga into Kriya will Unleash the most Powerful Yoga Ever.

— KUNDALINI EXPOSED

Disclosing the Cosmic Mystery of Kundalini.
The Ultimate Guide to Kundalini Yoga, Kundalini Awakening, Rising, and Reposing on its Hidden Throne.

— THE YOGA OF CONSCIOUSNESS

25 Direct Practices to Enlightenment.
Revealing the Missing Key to Self-Realization. Beyond Kundalini, Kriya Yoga & all Spirituality into Awakening Non-Duality.

— SAMADHI: THE FORGOTTEN EDEN

Unveiling the ancient art of how yogis and mystics had the keys to an unlimited reservoir of wisdom and power.
This book brings the timeless and forgotten wisdom of Samadhi into modern-day practicality.

Available @ Amazon as Kindle & Paperback.

GLOSSARY

Advaita Vedanta – Advaita means "not-two." Vedanta is the metaphysical philosophy and doctrine derived from the Upanishads, the final part of the Vedas. Advaita Vedanta is the school that explains those scriptures with a non-dual perspective. **Neo-Advaita** is a distortion of Advaita Vedanta. Proponents of Neo-Advaita teachings affirm that no practice is necessary and that having an enlightenment-experience is enough to be enlightened.

Ashramas – The four stages of life within the Hindu tradition based on ancient Indian texts.

Background of Consciousness / Witness – Another name for pure Awareness. However, such a name presupposes that there is a foreground or that which is witnessed, implying a duality. That's quite right, but it should be understood that this name is a helpful clue for seekers because it helps them take a step back from the mental contents with which they are usually identified, so that they can repose in awareness itself.

Brahman – The Ultimate Reality, the **Absolute**. Some call it **Parabrahman** or **Nirguna Brahman**, which means Highest Brahman or Brahman without form or qualities. It is the **Unmanifested**, which is Awareness devoid of all contents, pure and formless.

Beingness – The intrinsic nature of Consciousness is "Being." To be is to be conscious. At first, "Beingness" might be felt as a profound experience of stillness, peace, joy, etc., but as one goes further, it will dissolve our individuality, and our blissful Oneness will shine through. Refer to *Kundalini Exposed* and *The Yoga of Consciousness*.

Consciousness / Awareness – I use these terms interchangeably throughout this book. Our pure and true formless Self-aware nature. That which is conscious; Is your body conscious? No. Is your brain conscious? No. We could go on all day, until we realize that nothing is conscious by itself, except consciousness; what the whole *Real Yoga* series points toward.

Dynamic consciousness – The manifested side of Consciousness; the relative consciousness.

Ego – "I," the thought "I" or "I-ego." It is the erroneous belief of being a separate being or entity. For a more in-depth understanding, read *The Yoga of Consciousness*.

God – Although I have written God as "Himself," God is neither male nor female. God is not a person or an entity—that would make God limited. God is the all-pervading Consciousness, being formless, timeless and unborn. It is the infinite Awareness that each one of us possesses, and out of which everything is "made."

Grace – The "pull" of pure Awareness. Figuratively speaking, it's like an "intervention" from the "beyond" which speeds up our purification, awakening, and realization. The mind can't dissect Grace.

Kundalini – The primal spiritual energy said to be located at the base of the spine. **Cosmic Kundalini** is the same energy but rather than being the individual's latent energy, it is the universal latent energy, being infinitely more powerful. For a deeper understanding, read *Kundalini Exposed*.

Maya – The veil of illusion that appears to cover our true infinite nature. This veil allows pure empty consciousness to believe it has divided itself into many different forms, each with different qualities, from beings to thoughts to galaxies. It is the **manifested relative**: the contents of Awareness which have manifested from its infinite potential.

Mouna – The pure silence of Being, which is the emptiness of Self-Realization; Self-Awareness. It is a concept that conveys a different aspect of the same principle.

Nadis – The subtle channel through which the life-force flows; the nerves of the nervous system.

Parvastha – The "After-Kriya" blissful Self-Awareness state. This is the same state as being aware of being aware and of being present.

Prana – Life-force.

Pranayama – Life-force restraint/control technique.

Sadhana – Spiritual Practice.

Samadhi – Absorption; a higher state of consciousness.

Sannyasa – The fourth *ashrama* of Hinduism. People in this stage of life have renounced all connections with the world and live a life devoted to spiritual practice.

Satsang – Association with Being, or, alternatively, being in the presence of a Self-Realized Master.

Sattvic Conditioning – Pure conditioning such as compassion, balance, equilibrium, purity, etc.

Self – With a capital "S" means pure Consciousness or pure Awareness, devoid of any objects. Unless specified otherwise, in this book, awareness and consciousness are used interchangeably; self with a small "s" is synonymous with ego or "I."

Shakti – Personification of Kundalini, the life-force principle that gives life to the Universe.

Siddhis – Supernatural powers or abilities. Lots of seekers have the misconception that an enlightened being possesses a multitude of siddhis. This is both true and false.

It is false in the sense that an enlightened being is devoid of a personal self, and only a self-deluded person would believe in "I do this miracle," "I have this siddhi," "I have so-and-so superpower," etc. These are merely egoic statements. Furthermore, an enlightened being is not under the illusion of being a doer or performer of actions (including siddhis).

This is not to imply that enlightened beings don't possess any so-called "supernatural abilities," but if such powers or miracles are displayed, from the enlightened being's perspective, nothing was done to make them happen—these miracles happened on their own as a natural reflection of the pure state of the enlightened being. Just like the example in chapter 17 regarding the sun "being" and "doing," or when gravity pulls an apple toward the ground, siddhis happen without a performer. Hence, it can also be said to be true.

Lots of miracles have been reported to occur either physically near to an enlightened Master or with his/her blessing. Whenever you are bathed in the presence and grace of a genuine Master, you become more connected to your own true nature, by virtue of this association (*satsang*). The more you are connected to your true nature, the more "miracles" happen on their own.

This doesn't necessarily imply that you need to be in the physical presence of a true Master either. Their grace, presence, and guidance are not limited by space-time; they are ever-available, ever-present and ever pulling us back to our common source, the Self. It doesn't even matter if a Master is alive or not.

Of course, while an ignorant person might take credit for the siddhis, that would only be an illusion. Attempting to develop them is also freefalling into Maya's intricate web of trickery. It's that simple.

Read Chapter 1 "God is the True Siddhi" in *The Secret Power of Kriya Yoga* for a better understanding of the real and ultimate Siddhi. That's the one worth having!

Spiritual Heart – The rarely mentioned "void of nothingness." After the culmination in the thousand-petaled lotus, the Kundalini descends via this channel into the "Cave of the Heart," also known as the "void of nothingness," where it will repose and dissolve completely. Although the whole of creation is nothing but Consciousness, the original "point" from where it all emerged can be said to be the Spiritual Heart. With that being said, it is not a chakra, a "place" or even a "space," but rather the underlying primal boundless pure Consciousness that we really are. Refer to *Kundalini Exposed* chapter 12 for more information.

Subconscious mind – That which is beneath the conscious mind. Sometimes, it is also called the "unconscious."

Transcendental-I – The pure "I;" The enlightened "I" that does not perceive anything as separated from itself; It's the same as "I am," which is the purest expression of Being; The residue of a seemingly relative consciousness that remains in enlightened beings after they realize their true egoless nature so that they can live and operate in the world.

Turiya – "The Fourth;" what this book is all about. The natural and progressive integration of the Truth into our relative vehicle of expression.

Turiyatita – "Beyond the Fourth;" it can be seen in two ways:

1st - Due to our long habit of considering the states of wakefulness, dreaming and sleep as real, we call the state of Self-Realization "The Fourth." In fact, there is no fourth state, because once the fourth state is, it is the only state, and thus it loses its meaning as the fourth state, which means Turiya is Turiyatita; The Fourth is Beyond the Fourth.

2nd - Turiya integration level 4, where there isn't even the slightest superimposition of any apparent relative state. It's not even correct to call it "integration." It's the perspective of the Absolute, which is the only real perspective, although calling it perspective is not correct either.

Vasanas / Samskaras – Latent tendencies stored in the causal body, responsible for reincarnation. They can also mean subtle habits and desires, psychological imprints, mental impressions or deep buried emotional traumas, or all of these combined.

Made in the USA
Charleston, SC
31 December 2013

Made in the USA
Lexington, KY
14 June 2019